Design Patterns in Modern C++20

Reusable Approaches for Object-Oriented Software Design

Second Edition

Dmitri Nesteruk

Apress®

Design Patterns in Modern C++20: Reusable Approaches for
Object-Oriented Software Design

Dmitri Nesteruk
St. Petersburg, Russia

ISBN-13 (pbk): 978-1-4842-7294-7   ISBN-13 (electronic): 978-1-4842-7295-4
https://doi.org/10.1007/978-1-4842-7295-4

Managing Director, Apress Media LLC: Welmoed Spahr
Acquisitions Editor: Steve Anglin
Development Editor: Matthew Moodie
Coordinating Editor: Mark Powers

Cover designed by eStudioCalamar

Cover image by Clark van der Beken on Unsplash (www.unsplash.com)

Distributed to the book trade worldwide by Apress Media, LLC, 1 New York Plaza, New York, NY 10004, U.S.A. Phone 1-800-SPRINGER, fax (201) 348-4505, e-mail orders-ny@springer-sbm.com, or visit www.springeronline.com. Apress Media, LLC is a California LLC and the sole member (owner) is Springer Science + Business Media Finance Inc (SSBM Finance Inc). SSBM Finance Inc is a **Delaware** corporation.

For information on translations, please e-mail booktranslations@springernature.com; for reprint, paperback, or audio rights, please e-mail bookpermissions@springernature.com.

Apress titles may be purchased in bulk for academic, corporate, or promotional use. eBook versions and licenses are also available for most titles. For more information, reference our Print and eBook Bulk Sales web page at http://www.apress.com/bulk-sales.

Any source code or other supplementary material referenced by the author in this book is available to readers on GitHub via the book's product page, located at www.apress.com/9781484272947. For more detailed information, please visit http://www.apress.com/source-code.

Printed on acid-free paper

Table of Contents

About the Author

Dmitri Nesteruk is a quantitative analyst, developer, course and book author, and an occasional conference speaker. His professional interests lie in software development and integration practices in the areas of computation, quantitative finance, and algorithmic trading. His technological interests include C# and C++ programming as well as high-performance computing using technologies such as CUDA and FPGAs. He has been a C# MVP since 2009.

About the Technical Reviewers

David Pazmino has been developing software applications for 20 years in Fortune 100 companies. He is an experienced developer in front-end and back-end development who specializes in developing machine learning models for financial applications. David has developed many applications in C++, STL, and ATL for companies using Microsoft technologies. He currently develops applications in Scala and Python for deep learning neural networks. David has a degree from Cornell University, a masters from Pace University in Computer Science, and a masters from Northwestern in Predictive Analytics.

Massimo Nardone has more than 25 years of experience in security, web/mobile development, cloud, and IT architecture. His true IT passions are security and Android. He has been programming and teaching how to program with Android, Perl, PHP, Java, VB, Python, C/C++, and MySQL for more than 20 years. He holds a Master of Science degree in Computing Science from the University of Salerno, Italy.

He has worked as a CISO, CSO, security executive, IoT executive, project manager, software engineer, research engineer, chief security architect, PCI/SCADA auditor, and senior lead IT security/cloud/SCADA architect for many years. His technical skills include security, Android, cloud, Java, MySQL, Drupal, Cobol, Perl, web and mobile development, MongoDB, D3, Joomla, Couchbase, C/C++, WebGL, Python, Pro Rails, Django CMS, Jekyll, Scratch, and more.

He worked as visiting lecturer and supervisor for exercises at the Networking Laboratory of the Helsinki University of Technology (Aalto University). He holds four international patents (PKI, SIP, SAML, and Proxy areas). He is currently working for Cognizant as head of cyber security and CISO to help both internally and externally with clients in areas of information and cyber security, like strategy, planning, processes, policies, procedures, governance, awareness, and so forth. In June 2017 he became a permanent member of the ISACA Finland Board.

Massimo has reviewed more than 45 IT books for different publishing companies and is the co-author of *Pro Spring Security: Securing Spring Framework 5 and Boot 2-based Java Applications* (Apress, 2019), *Beginning EJB in Java EE 8* (Apress, 2018), *Pro JPA 2 in Java EE 8* (Apress, 2018), and *Pro Android Games* (Apress, 2015).

CHAPTER 1

Introduction

The topic of design patterns sounds dry, academically dull, and, in all honesty, done to death in almost every programming language imaginable – including programming languages such as JavaScript which aren't even properly OOP! So why another book on it? I know that if you're reading this, you probably have a limited amount of time to decide whether this book is worth the investment.

The main reason why this book exists is that C++ is "great again." After a long period of stagnation, it's now evolving and growing, and, despite the fact that it has to contend with backward C compatibility, good things are happening – they may not always happen at the pace we'd all like, but this is a byproduct of the way the evolution of the C++ language standard is structured.

Now, on to design patterns – we shouldn't forget that the original *Design Patterns* book[1] was published with examples in C++ and Smalltalk. Since then, plenty of programming languages have incorporated design patterns directly into the language: for example, C# directly incorporated the Observer pattern with its built-in support for events (and the corresponding `event` keyword). C++ has *not* done the same, at least not on the syntax level. That said, the introduction of types such as `std::function` sure made things a lot simpler for many programming scenarios.

---

[1] Erich Gamma et al. (1994), *Design Patterns: Elements of Reusable Object-Oriented Software*, Addison-Wesley

© Dmitri Nesteruk 2022
D. Nesteruk, *Design Patterns in Modern C++20*,
https://doi.org/10.1007/978-1-4842-7295-4_1

Design patterns are also a fun investigation of how a particular problem can be solved in many different ways, with varying degrees of technical sophistication and different sorts of trade-offs. Some patterns are more or less essential and unavoidable, whereas other patterns are more of a scientific curiosity (but nevertheless will be discussed in this book, since I'm a completionist).

Readers should be aware that comprehensive solutions to certain problems (e.g., the Observer pattern) typically result in overengineering, that is, the creation of structures that are far more complicated than is necessary for most typical scenarios. While overengineering is a lot of fun (hey, you get to solve the problem *and* impress your coworkers), it's often not feasible in the real world of time and budgeting constraints.

Who This Book Is For

This book is intended to be a modern-day update to the classic GoF book, targeting specifically the C++ programming language. I mean, how many of you are writing Smalltalk out there? Not many, that would be my guess.[2]

The goal of this book is to investigate how we can apply Modern C++ (the latest versions of C++ currently available) to the implementations of classic design patterns. At the same time, it's also an attempt to flesh out any new patterns and approaches that could be useful to C++ developers.

Finally, in some places, this book is quite simply a technology demo for Modern C++, showcasing how some of its latest features (e.g., concepts) make difficult problems a lot easier to solve.

---

[2] To be fair, the Pharo variety of Smalltalk has some interesting ideas that I have since borrowed and adapted to other programming languages. One idea, which I managed to successfully transplant, is the idea of input-output matching. It works like this: you give the software desired input and output values, say, abc and 3, and a piece of software uses combinatorial analysis to derive the expression `x.length()` for taking you from one to another.

On Code Examples

The examples in this book are all suitable for putting into production, but a few simplifications have been made in order to aid readability:

- Quite often, you'll find me using a `struct` instead of a `class` in order to avoid writing the `public` keyword in too many places.

- I will avoid the `std::` prefix, as it can hurt readability, especially in places where code density is high. If I'm using `string`, you can be sure I'm referring to `std::string`.

- I will avoid adding virtual destructors, whereas, in real life, it might make sense to add them in certain places.

- In some cases, I create and pass parameters by value to avoid the proliferation of `shared_ptr/make_shared/etc`. Smart pointers add another level of complexity, and their integration into the design patterns presented in this book is often left as an exercise for the reader.

- I will sometimes omit code elements that would otherwise be necessary for feature-completing a type (e.g., move constructors) as those take up too much space. Feature-completing a type is quite often a separate challenge, somewhat unrelated to the topic at hand.

- There will be plenty of cases where I will omit `const`, whereas, under normal circumstances, it would actually make sense to use it. Const-correctness quite often causes a split and a doubling of the API surface, something that doesn't work well in book format.

3

You should be aware that most of the examples leverage Modern C++ (C++ 14, 17, 20, and beyond) and generally use the latest C++ language features that are available to developers at the time of writing. For example, you won't find many function signatures ending in `-> decltype(...)` when C++14 lets us automatically infer the return type. None of the examples target a particular compiler, but if something doesn't work with your chosen compiler,[3] you'll need to find workarounds.

At certain points in time, I will be referring to other programming languages such as C# or Kotlin. It is often interesting to note how designers of other languages have implemented a particular feature. C++ is no stranger to borrowing generally available ideas from other languages: for example, the introduction of `auto` and type inference on variable declarations and return types is present in many other languages.

On Developer Tools

The code samples in this book were written to work with Modern C++ compilers, such as Clang, GCC, and MSVC. I make the general assumption that you are using the latest compiler version that is available and thus will use the latest and greatest language features that are available to me. In some cases, the advanced language examples will need to be downgraded for earlier compilers; in others, it might not work out. Naturally, if I use any experimental language features, they might not work in all compilers until they catch up to the necessary level of C++ language support.

As far as developer tools are concerned, this book does not focus on them specifically, so, provided you have an up-to-date compiler, you should follow the examples just fine: most of them are self-contained

---

[3] Plenty of compilers, such as the Intel C++ Compiler, do not make it their goal to support all features of a particular C++ standard as quickly as possible. Nevertheless, these compilers do have their own loyal followings because they shine in areas other than feature-completeness such as optimization.

single .cpp files, but some examples that involve complex dependencies or static initialization are spread across several files. Regardless, I'd like to take this opportunity to remind you that quality developer tools such as CLion or ReSharper C++ greatly improve the development experience. For a tiny amount of money that you invest, you get a wealth of additional functionality that directly translates to improvements in coding speed and the quality of the code produced.

Preface to the Second Edition

The world is changing. Some of those changes, such as the pandemic that we're currently experiencing worldwide, are a bit frightening. On the other hand, some changes are good: the C++20 standard has finally been ratified, and C++20 language features such as modules and concepts are making an appearance in popular C++ compilers.

We are, of course, far from having a complete implementation in any given compiler. For example, even if we are able to use modules in our own code, we still need to wait in order to have modularized implementations of the Standard Library, Boost, and other popular libraries. But what we have right now is already changing the way design patterns are implemented. For example, if, in the past, we wanted to ensure a template argument implemented some interface, we would use a `static_assert`. But now, with C++20, we can leverage concepts, which are reusable (avoiding cut and paste) and self-descriptive.

With the never-ending evolution of C++, we can all feel as if we were on a never-ending journey that keeps getting better and better. The only challenge is to learn how to leverage all the new functionality, a challenge for which I hope this book can become a useful tool. Enjoy!

Important Concepts

Before we begin, I wanted to briefly mention some of the key concepts of the C++ world that will be referenced in this book. None of them are particularly advanced, and most of them will be familiar to experienced C++ developers.

Curiously Recurring Template Pattern

I don't know if it qualifies to be listed as a separate *design* pattern, but the curiously recurring template pattern (CRTP) is certainly a pattern of sorts in the C++ world. The idea is simple: an inheritor passes *itself* as a template argument to its base class.

```cpp
struct Foo : SomeBase<Foo>
{
  ...
}
```

Why would one ever do that? Well, one reason is to be able to access a typed this pointer inside a base class implementation.

For example, suppose every single inheritor of SomeBase implements a begin()/end() pair required for iteration. How can you iterate the object inside a member of SomeBase, rather than inside the inheritor class? Intuition suggests that you cannot, because SomeBase itself does not provide a begin()/end() interface. But if you use CRTP, a derived class can pass information about *itself* to the base class:

```cpp
struct MyClass : SomeBase<MyClass>
{
  class iterator {
```

```
    // your iterator defined here
  }
  iterator begin() const { ... }
  iterator end() const { ... }
}
```

This means that, inside the base class, you can cast this to a derived class type:

```
template <typename Derived>
struct SomeBase
{
  void foo()
  {
    for (auto& item : *static_cast<Derived*>(this))
    {
      ...
    }
  }
}
```

When calling foo() on an instance of MyClass, this pointer gets cast from SomeBase* to MyClass*. We then dereference the pointer and iterate on it using a range-based for loop which, of course, calls MyClass::begin() and MyClass::end() behind the scenes.

For a concrete example of this approach, check out Chapter 8, "Composite."

Mixin Inheritance

In C++, a class can be defined to inherit from its own template argument, that is:

```
template <typename T> struct Mixin : T
{
  ...
}
```

This approach is called *mixin inheritance* and allows hierarchical composition of types. For example, you can make an instance of Foo<Bar<Baz>> x; that implements the traits of all three classes, without having to actually construct a brand new FooBarBaz type.

Mixin inheritance is particularly useful together with Concepts because it allows us to put constraints on the type our mixin inherits from and lets us deterministically use the base type features without relying on compile-time errors to tell us we are doing something wrong.

For a concrete example of this approach, check out Chapter 9, "Decorator."

Old-Fashioned Static Polymorphism

Imagine you want to build an alert system that notifies someone about an event by different means: email, SMS, Telegram, etc. Under the CRTP paradigm, you could implement a base Notifier class similar to the following:

```
template <typename TImpl>
class Notifier {
public:
```

```
  void AlertSMS(string_view msg)
  {
    impl().SendAlertSMS(msg);
  }
  void AlertEmail(string_view msg)
  {
    impl().SendAlertEmail(msg);
  }
private:
  TImpl& impl() { return static_cast<TImpl&>(*this); }
  friend TImpl;
};
```

Since TImpl is a template argument, we can call methods on it with impunity, knowing that, even though we're not explicitly specifying that TImpl must inherit from Notifier (we'll do this soon enough), the compiler will check that the methods AlertSMS() and AlertEmail() do actually exist.

This allows us to define a method which sends an alert on all channels:

```
template <typename TImpl>
void AlertAllChannels(Notifier<TImpl>& notifier, string_view
msg)
{
  notifier.AlertEmail(msg);
  notifier.AlertSMS(msg);
}
```

Now all that remains is to construct implementations of `Notifier`. For example, you can build a no-op (see the Null Object pattern) notifier for testing:

```
struct TestNotifier: public Notifier<TestNotifier>
{
  void SendAlertSMS(string_view msg){}
  void SendAlertEmail(string_view msg){}
};
```

And you can use this to do absolutely nothing!

```
TestNotifier tn;
AlertAllChannels(tn, "testing!"); // just testing!
```

While this is a workable approach, it has deficiencies, namely:

- We end up having two parallel APIs, that is, `AlertSMS()`/`SendAlertSMS()`. We cannot call those methods the same because then one would hide another (and your IDE will complain).

- The whole `impl()` thing is weird and feels unnecessary. You'd expect the alert methods to be virtual in base class and overriding in the implementing class.

- There's no explicit enforcement that `TImpl` has any particular interface; we try to call things to check them at runtime, but the implementer is not informed about what we call and where. Concepts can help with this.

Static Polymorphism with Concepts

The solution here is to introduce a concept that requires the presence of relevant member functions:

```cpp
template <typename TImpl>
concept IsANotifier = requires(TImpl impl) {
  impl.AlertSMS(string_view{});
  impl.AlertEmail(string_view{});
};
```

Now, we no longer need the base Notifier class: we can simply construct the AlertAllChannels method that expects some type that has all the AlertXxx() methods:

```cpp
template <IsANotifier TImpl>
void AlertAllChannels(TImpl& impl, string_view msg)
{
  impl.AlertSMS(msg);
  impl.AlertEmail(msg);
}
```

In this function, the TImpl template argument is required to support the IsANotifier concept. We can make a class that conforms to this requirement:

```cpp
struct TestNotifier
{
  void AlertSMS(string_view msg) {}
  void AlertEmail(string_view msg) {}
};
```

And continue to use it as before. As you can see, we avoid the notion of a base class altogether.

Properties

Properties are a topic worth mentioning even though they are not part of the C++ standard. Despite the fact that properties have already proven themselves over and over in other programming languages, many C++ programming purists continue to believe that they have no business being part of C++ and are best implemented as a library solution – something that doesn't work particularly well, to be honest.

A *property* is nothing more than a (typically private) field and a combination of a getter and a setter. In standard C++, a property looks as follows:

```
class Person
{
  int age;
public:
  int get_age() const { return age; }
  void set_age(int value) { age = value; }
};
```

Plenty of languages (e.g., C#, Kotlin) internalize the notion of a property by baking it directly into the programming language. While C++ has not done this (and is unlikely to do so anytime in the future), there is a non-standard declaration specifier called `property` that you can use in most compilers (MSVC, Clang, Intel):

```
class Person
{
```

```
  int age_;
public:
  int get_age() const { return age_; }
  void set_age(int value) { age_ = value; }
  __declspec(property(get=get_age, put=set_age)) int age;
};
```

What happens here is, within `__declspec(property(...))` field declaration, you specify the getter and the setter using the keywords get and put. This then becomes a virtual field – it doesn't result in any memory allocations, but attempts to access this field or write to it are replaced by the compiler with calls to the getter and setter, respectively.

This can be used as follows:

```
Person p;
p.age = 20; // calls p.set_age(20)
```

Those not fond of C++ language extensions typically expose properties as a combination of getter and setter methods, often by keeping the field private and exposing a pair of identically named (overloaded) methods with the same name as the field they expose:

```
class Person
{
  int _age;
public:
  int age() const { return _age; }
  void age(int value) { _age = value; }
}
```

Why is this discussion relevant? In and of themselves, getters and setters may seem useless: if you have a field that you want people to modify, expose it as public and be done with it! If, however, you want to perform additional actions – for example, notifying subscribers that a field has changed – then the setter is exactly the place where some of the code should go. This is what we'll encounter when we talk about the Observer design pattern.

The SOLID Design Principles

SOLID is an acronym which stands for the following design principles (and their abbreviations):

- Single Responsibility Principle (SRP)

- Open-Closed Principle (OCP)

- Liskov Substitution Principle (LSP)

- Interface Segregation Principle (ISP)

- Dependency Inversion Principle (DIP)

These principles were introduced by Robert C. Martin in the early 2000s – in fact, they are just a selection of five principles out of dozens that are expressed in Robert's books and his blog.[4] These five particular topics permeate the discussion of patterns and software design in general, so before we dive into design patterns (I know you're all eager to see them), we're going to do a brief recap of what the SOLID principles are all about.

---

[4] https://blog.cleancoder.com/

Single Responsibility Principle

Suppose you decide to keep a journal of your most intimate thoughts. The journal has a title and a number of entries. You could model it as follows:

```
struct Journal
{
  string title;
  vector<string> entries;

  explicit Journal(const string& title) : title{title} {}
};
```

Now, you could add functionality for adding an entry to the journal, prefixed by the entry's ordinal number in the journal. This is easy:

```
void Journal::add(const string& entry)
{
  static int count = 1;
  entries.push_back(boost::lexical_cast<string>(count++)
    + ": " + entry);
}
```

And the journal is now usable as

```
Journal j{"Dear Diary"};
j.add("I cried today");
j.add("I ate a bug");
```

It makes sense to have this function as part of the Journal class because adding a journal entry is something the journal actually needs to do. It is the journal's responsibility to keep entries, so anything related to that is fair game.

Now suppose you decide to make the journal persist by saving it in a file. You add this code to the `Journal` class:

```cpp
void Journal::save(const string& filename)
{
  ofstream ofs(filename);
  for (auto& s : entries)
    ofs << s << endl;
}
```

This approach is problematic. The journal's responsibility is to *keep* journal entries, not to write them to disk. If you add the disk-writing functionality to `Journal` and similar classes, any change in the approach to persistence (say, you decide to write to the cloud instead of disk) would require lots of tiny changes in each of the affected classes.

I want to pause here and make a point: a situation that leads us to having to do lots of tiny changes in lots of classes, whether related (as in a hierarchy) or not, is typically a *code smell* – an indication that something's not quite right. Now, it really depends on the situation: if we're renaming a symbol that's being used in a hundred places, I'd argue that's generally OK because ReSharper, CLion, or whatever IDE we use will actually let us perform a refactoring and have the change propagate everywhere. But when we need to completely rework an interface... well, this can be a very painful process!

We therefore state that persistence is a separate concern, one that is better expressed in a separate class, for example:

```cpp
struct PersistenceManager
{
  static void save(const Journal& j, const string& filename)
```

```
  {
    ofstream ofs(filename);
    for (auto& s : j.entries)
      ofs << s << endl;
  }
};
```

And this is precisely what we mean by *Single Responsibility*: each class has only one responsibility and therefore has only one reason to change. Journal would need to change only if there's something more that needs to be done with respect to storage of entries – for example, we might want each entry prefixed by a timestamp, so we would change the add() function to do exactly that. On the other hand, if we wanted to change the persistence mechanic, this would be changed in PersistenceManager.

An extreme example of an anti-pattern[5] that violates the SRP is called a *God Object*. A God Object is a huge class that tries to handle as many concerns as possible, becoming a monolithic monstrosity that is very difficult to work with.

Luckily for us, God Objects are easy to recognize and, thanks to source control systems (just count the number of member functions), the responsible developer can be quickly identified and adequately punished.

Open-Closed Principle

Suppose we have an (entirely hypothetical) range of products in a database. Each product has a color and size and is defined as

---

[5] An *anti-pattern* is a design pattern that also, unfortunately, shows up in code often enough to be recognized globally. The difference between a pattern and an anti-pattern is that anti-patterns are common examples of *bad* design, resulting in code that's difficult to understand, maintain, and refactor.

```
enum class Color { Red, Green, Blue };
enum class Size { Small, Medium, Large };

struct Product
{
  string name;
  Color color;
  Size size;
};
```

Now, we want to provide certain filtering capabilities for a given set of products. We make a filter similar to the following:

```
struct ProductFilter
{
  typedef vector<Product*> Items;
};
```

Now, to support filtering products by color, we define a member function to do exactly that:

```
ProductFilter::Items ProductFilter::by_color(
  Items items, Color color)
{
  Items result;
  for (auto& i : items)
    if (i->color == color)
      result.push_back(i);
  return result;
}
```

Our current approach of filtering items by color is fine. Our code goes into production, but, sometime later, the boss comes in and asks us to implement filtering by size too. So, we jump back into `ProductFilter.cpp`, add the following code, and recompile:

```
ProductFilter::Items ProductFilter::by_size(
  Items items, Size size)
{
  Items result;
  for (auto& i : items)
    if (i->size == size)
      result.push_back(i);
  return result;
}
```

This feels like outright duplication, doesn't it? Why don't we just write a general method that takes a predicate (a `bool`-returning `std::function`)? Well, one reason could be that different forms of filtering can be done in different ways: for example, some record types might be indexed and need to be searched in a specific way; some data types may be amenable to search on a GPU while others are not.

Our code goes into production, but, once again, the boss comes back and tells us that now there's a need to search by both color *and* size. So what are we to do but add another function?

```
ProductFilter::Items ProductFilter::by_color_and_size(
  Items items, Size size, Color color)
{
  Items result;
```

```
  for (auto& i : items)
    if (i->size == size && i->color == color)
      result.push_back(i);
  return result;
}
```

What we want from this scenario is to enforce the *Open-Closed Principle* that states that a type is open for extension but closed for modification. In other words, we want filtering that is extensible (perhaps in a different compilation unit) without having to modify it (and recompiling something that already works and may have been shipped to clients).

How can we achieve this? Well, first of all, we conceptually separate (SRP!) our filtering process into two parts: a filter (a process which takes all items and only returns some) and a specification (the definition of a predicate to apply to a data element).

We can make a very simple definition of a specification interface:

```
template <typename T> struct Specification
{
  virtual bool is_satisfied(T* item) = 0;
};
```

In the preceding, type T is whatever we choose it to be: it can certainly be a Product, but it can also be something else. This makes the entire approach reusable.

Next, we need a way of filtering based on Specification<T>. This is done by defining, you guessed it, a Filter<T>:

```
template <typename T> struct Filter
```

```
{
  virtual vector<T*> filter(
    vector<T*> items,
    Specification<T>& spec) const = 0;
};
```

Again, all we are doing is specifying the signature for a function called filter which takes all the items and a specification and returns all items that conform to the specification. There is an assumption that the items are stored as a vector<T*>, but in reality, you could pass filter() either a pair of iterators or some custom-made interface designed specifically for going through a collection. Regrettably, the C++ language has failed to standardize the notion of an enumeration or collection, something that exists in other programming languages (e.g., .NET's IEnumerable).

Based on the preceding, the implementation of an improved filter is simple:

```
struct BetterFilter : Filter<Product>
{
  vector<Product*> filter(
    vector<Product*> items,
    Specification<Product>& spec) override
  {
    vector<Product*> result;
    for (auto& p : items)
      if (spec.is_satisfied(p))
        result.push_back(p);
    return result;
  }
};
```

You can think of a Specification<T> that's being passed in as a strongly typed equivalent of an std::function that is constrained only to a certain number of possible filter specifications.

Now, here's the easy part. To make a color filter, you make a ColorSpecification:

```cpp
struct ColorSpecification : Specification<Product>
{
  Color color;

  explicit ColorSpecification(const Color color) : color{color} {}

  bool is_satisfied(Product* item) override {
    return item->color == color;
  }
};
```

Armed with this specification, and given a list of products, we can now filter them as follows:

```cpp
Product apple{ "Apple", Color::Green, Size::Small };
Product tree{ "Tree", Color::Green, Size::Large };
Product house{ "House", Color::Blue, Size::Large };

vector<Product*> all{ &apple, &tree, &house };

BetterFilter bf;
ColorSpecification green(Color::Green);

auto green_things = bf.filter(all, green);
for (auto& x : green_things)
  cout << x->name << " is green";
```

This code finds "Apple" and "Tree" because they are both green. Now, the only thing we haven't implemented so far is searching for size *and* color (or, indeed, explained how you would search for size *or* color, or mix different criteria). The answer is that you simply make a specification *combinator*. For example, for the logical AND, you can make it as follows:[6]

```
template <typename T> struct AndSpecification :
Specification<T>
{
  Specification<T>& first;
  Specification<T>& second;

  AndSpecification(Specification<T>& first,
    Specification<T>& second)
    : first{first}, second{second} {}

  bool is_satisfied(T* item) override
  {
    return first.is_satisfied(item) && second.is_satisfied(item);
  }
};
```

And now, you are free to create composite conditions on the basis of simpler Specifications. Reusing the green specification we made earlier, finding something green and big is now as simple as

```
SizeSpecification large(Size::Large);
ColorSpecification green(Color::Green);
AndSpecification<Product> green_and_large{ large, green };
```

---

[6] The choice to store polymorphic references here is completely arbitrary and is a bit of a trade-off. It's easy to implement, but you lose an ability to store by value. One alternative is to use smart pointers, but this makes the implementation a lot more complicated.

```
auto big_green_things = bf.filter(all, green_and_big);
for (auto& x : big_green_things)
  cout << x->name << " is large and green";
// Tree is large and green
```

That was a lot of code and quite a few data structures that we've created – take a look at Figure 1-1 for a visual illustration!

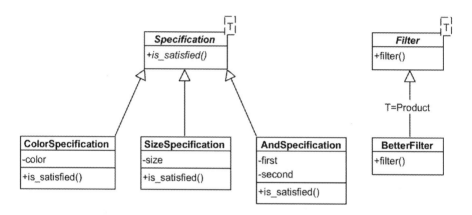

Figure 1-1. *Specification pattern class diagram*

Plenty of embellishments are, of course, possible. For example, thanks to the power of C++, you can simply introduce an operator && for two Specification<T> objects, thereby making the process of filtering by two (or more!) criteria extremely simple:

```
template <typename T> struct Specification
{
  virtual bool is_satisfied(T* item) = 0;
```

```
AndSpecification<T> operator &&(Specification& other)
{
    return AndSpecification<T>(*this, other);
}
};
```

Of course, post hoc addition of an operator violates OCP, so as an alternative, you – or the client using `Specification` – can add an operator on the global scope later on:

```
template <typename T> AndSpecification<T> operator&&
  (const Specification<T>& first,
   const Specification<T>& second)
{
  return { first, second };
}
```

This can shorten our example just a little:

```
SizeSpecification large(Size::Large);
ColorSpecification green(Color::Green);

auto big_green_things = bf.filter(all, green && large);
for (auto& x : big_green_things)
  cout << x->name << " is large and green" << endl;
```

Sadly, you still cannot write a one-liner similar to the following:

```
auto green_and_big =
  ColorSpecification(Color::Green)
  && SizeSpecification(Size::Large);
```

because these temporaries will die and the constructor does not prolong their lifetime. There are ways to make this work, but this is outside the scope of our present discussion.

So let's recap what the OCP is and how this example enforces it. Basically, OCP states that you shouldn't need to go back to code you've already written and tested, and change it. And that's exactly the guideline we're following here! We made `Specification<T>` and `Filter<T>` and, from then on, all we have to do is implement either of the interfaces (without modifying the interfaces themselves) to implement new filtering mechanics. This is what is meant by "open for extension, closed for modification."

Liskov Substitution Principle

The Liskov Substitution Principle, named after Barbara Liskov, states that if an interface takes an object of type `Parent`, it should equally take an object of type `Child` without anything breaking. Let's take a look at a situation where LSP is broken.

Here's a rectangle; it has width and height and a bunch of getters and setters calculating the area:

```
class Rectangle
{
protected:
  int width, height;
public:
  Rectangle(const int width, const int height)
    : width{width}, height{height} { }

  int get_width() const { return width; }
  virtual void set_width(const int width) { this->width = width; }
```

```
  int get_height() const { return height; }
  virtual void set_height(const int height) { this->height =
  height; }

  int area() const { return width * height; }
};
```

Now let's suppose we make a special kind of Rectangle called a Square. This object overrides the setters to set both width *and* height:

```
class Square : public Rectangle
{
public:
  Square(int size): Rectangle(size,size) {}
  void set_width(const int width) override {
    this->width = height = width;
  }
  void set_height(const int height) override {
    this->height = width = height;
  }
};
```

This approach is *evil*. You cannot see it yet, because it looks very innocent indeed: the setters simply set both dimensions, what could possibly go wrong? Well, we can easily construct a function taking a Rectangle that would blow up when taking a square:

```
void process(Rectangle& r)
{
  int w = r.get_width();
  r.set_height(10);
```

```
  cout << "expected area = " << (w * 10)
    << ", got " << r.area() << endl;
}
```

This function takes the formula Area = Width × Height as an invariant. It gets the width, sets the height, and rightly expects the product to be equal to the calculated area. But calling this function with a Square yields a mismatch:

```
Square s{5};
process(s); // expected area = 50, got 25
```

The takeaway from this example (which I admit is a little contrived) is that process() breaks the LSP by being thoroughly unable to take a derived type Square instead of the base type Rectangle. If you feed it a Rectangle, everything is fine, so it might take some time before the problem shows up in your tests (or in production – hopefully not!).

What's the solution? Well, there are many. Personally, I'd argue that the type Square shouldn't even exist: instead, we can make a Factory (see Chapter 3, "Factories") that creates both rectangles and squares:

```
struct RectangleFactory
{
  static Rectangle create_rectangle(int w, int h);
  static Rectangle create_square(int size);
};
```

You might also want a way of detecting that a Rectangle is, in fact, a square:

```
bool Rectangle::is_square() const
{
  return width == height;
}
```

The nuclear option, in this case, would be to throw an exception in Square's set_width()/set_height(), stating that these operations are unsupported and you should be using set_size() instead. This, however, violates the *principle of least surprise*, since you would expect a call to set_width() to make a meaningful change... am I right?

Interface Segregation Principle

Oh-kay, here is another contrived example that is nonetheless suitable for illustrating the problem. Suppose you decide to define a multifunction printer: a device that can print, scan, and also fax documents. So you define it like so:

```
struct MyFavouritePrinter /* : IMachine */
{
  void print(vector<Document*> docs) override;
  void fax(vector<Document*> docs) override;
  void scan(vector<Document*> docs) override;
};
```

This is fine. Now, suppose you decide to define an interface that needs to be implemented by everyone who also plans to make a multifunction printer. So you could use the Extract Interface function in your favorite IDE and you'll get something like the following:

```
struct IMachine
{
  virtual void print(vector<Document*> docs) = 0;
```

```
  virtual void fax(vector<Document*> docs) = 0;
  virtual void scan(vector<Document*> docs) = 0;
};
```

This is a problem. The reason it is a problem is that some implementer of this interface might not need scanning or faxing, just printing. And yet, you are forcing them to implement those extra features: sure, they can all be no-op, but why bother with this?

So what the Interface Segregation Principle suggests is you split up interfaces so that implementers can pick and choose depending on their needs. Since printing and scanning are different operations (e.g., a scanner cannot print), we define separate interfaces for these:

```
struct IPrinter
{
  virtual void print(vector<Document*> docs) = 0;
};
```

```
struct IScanner
{
  virtual void scan(vector<Document*> docs) = 0;
};
```

Then, a printer or a scanner can just implement the required functionality:

```
struct Printer : IPrinter
{
  void print(vector<Document*> docs) override;
};
```

```
struct Scanner : IScanner
{
  void scan(vector<Document*> docs) override;
};
```

Now, if we really want an IMachine interface, we can define it as a combination of the aforementioned interfaces:

```
struct IMachine: IPrinter, IScanner /* IFax and so on */
{
};
```

And when you come to implement this interface in your concrete multifunction device, this is the interface to use. For example, you could use simple delegation to ensure that Machine reuses the functionality provided by a particular IPrinter and IScanner:

```
struct Machine : IMachine
{
  IPrinter& printer;
  IScanner& scanner;

  Machine(IPrinter& printer, IScanner& scanner)
    : printer{printer},
      scanner{scanner}
  {
  }

  void print(vector<Document*> docs) override {
    printer.print(docs);
  }
```

```
void scan(vector<Document*> docs) override
{
  scanner.scan(docs);
}
};
```

In much the same vein, if you introduced an additional interface (say, IFax), you could incorporate it as part of the decorator. The entire set of classes is shown in Figure 1-2.

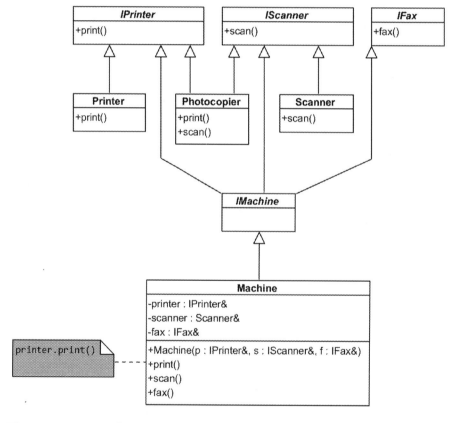

Figure 1-2. *Interface Segregation Principle class diagram*

So, just to recap, the idea here is to segregate parts of a complicated interface into separate interfaces so as to avoid forcing implementers to implement functionality that they do not really need. Anytime when you write a plug-in for some complicated application and you're given an interface with 20 confusing functions to implement with various no-ops and `return nullptr`, more likely than not the API authors have violated the ISP.

Dependency Inversion Principle

The original definition of the Dependency Inversion Principle states the following:[7]

A. *High-level modules should not depend on low-level modules. Both should depend on abstractions.*

What this statement essentially means is that if you're interested in logging, your reporting component should not depend on a concrete `ConsoleLogger`, but can depend on an `ILogger` interface. In this case, we are considering the reporting component to be high level (closer to the business domain), whereas logging, being a fundamental concern (kind of like file I/O or threading, but not quite), is considered a low-level module.

B. *Abstractions should not depend on details. Details should depend on abstractions.*

This is, once again, restating that depending on interfaces or base classes is better than depending on concrete types. Hopefully, the truth of this statement

---

[7] Martin, Robert C. (2003), *Agile Software Development, Principles, Patterns, and Practices*, Prentice Hall, pp. 127–131

is obvious, because such an approach supports better
configurability and testability, especially when you're
using a good framework to handle these dependencies
for you.

So, now, the main question is: how do we satisfy all of these requirements?
It sure is a lot more work, because now you need to explicitly state that, for
example, a Reporting component depends on an ILogger interface. The
way you would express it is perhaps as follows:

```
class Reporting
{
  ILogger& logger;
public:
  Reporting(const ILogger& logger) : logger{logger} {}
  void prepare_report()
  {
    logger.log_info("Preparing the report");
    ...
  }
};
}
```

The problem is that, to initialize this class, we would need to
explicitly call Reporting{ConsoleLogger{}} or something similar. And
what if Reporting is dependent upon five different interfaces? What if
ConsoleLogger has dependencies of its own? We *can* manage this by
writing a lot of code, but there is a better way.

The modern, trendy, fashionable way of doing this is to use *dependency injection*: this essentially means using a library such as Boost.DI[8] to *automatically* satisfy the dependency requirements for a particular component.

Let's consider an example of a car which has an engine, but also needs to write to a log. As it stands, we can say that a car *depends on* both of these things. To start with, we may define an engine as

```
struct Engine
{
  float volume = 5;
  int horse_power = 400;

  friend ostream& operator<< (ostream& os, const Engine& obj)
  {
    return os
      << "volume: " << obj.volume
      << " horse_power: " << obj.horse_power;
  } // thanks, ReSharper!
};
```

Now, it's up to us to decide whether or not we want to extract an IEngine interface and feed it to the car. Maybe we do, maybe we don't, and this is typically a design decision. If you envision having a hierarchy of engines, or you foresee needing a NullEngine (see the Null Object pattern) for testing purposes, then yes, you do need to abstract away the interfaces.

At any rate, we also want logging, and since this can be done in many ways (console, email, SMS, pigeon mail, etc.), we probably want to have an ILogger interface

---

[8] At the moment, Boost.DI is not yet part of Boost proper; it is part of the boost-experimental GitHub repository.

```
struct ILogger
{
  virtual ~ILogger() {}
  virtual void Log(const string& s) = 0;
};
```

as well as some sort of concrete implementation:

```
struct ConsoleLogger : ILogger
{

  ConsoleLogger() {}

  void Log(const string& s) override
  {
    cout << "LOG: " << s.c_str() << endl;
  }
};
```

Now, the car we're about to define depends on both the engine *and* the logging component. We need both, but it's really up to us how to store them: we can use a pointer, reference, a unique_ptr/shared_ptr, or something else. We shall define both of the dependent components as constructor parameters:

```
struct Car
{
  unique_ptr<Engine> engine;
  shared_ptr<ILogger> logger;

  Car(unique_ptr<Engine> engine,
      const shared_ptr<ILogger>& logger)
    : engine{move(engine)},
```

```
      logger{logger}
  {
    logger->Log("making a car");
  }
  friend ostream& operator<<(ostream& os, const Car& obj)
  {
    return os << "car with engine: " << *obj.engine;
  }
};
```

Now, you're probably expecting to see make_unique/make_shared calls as we initialize the Car. But we won't do any of that. Instead, we'll use Boost.DI. First of all, we'll define a binding that binds ILogger to ConsoleLogger; what this means is, basically, "any time someone asks for an ILogger give them a ConsoleLogger":

```
auto injector = di::make_injector(
  di::bind<ILogger>().to<ConsoleLogger>()
);
```

And now that we've configured the injector, we can use it to create a car:

```
auto car = injector.create<shared_ptr<Car>>();
```

This creates a `shared_ptr<Car>` that points to a *fully initialized* Car object, which is exactly what we wanted. The great thing about this approach is that to change the type of logger being used, we can change it in a single place (the `bind` call) and every place where an `ILogger` appears can now be using some other logging component that we provide. This approach also helps us with unit testing and allows us to use stubs (or the Null Object pattern) instead of mocks.

Alright, with the understanding of the SOLID design principles, we are now ready to take a look at the design patterns themselves!

PART I

Creational Patterns

Even in the absence of Creational patterns, the act of creating an object in C++ is fraught with peril. Should we create it on the stack or on the heap? Should we use a raw pointer, a unique or shared pointer, or something else entirely? Finally, is creating objects manually still kosher, or should we instead defer the creation of all key aspects of our infrastructure to specialized constructs such as Factories (more on them in just a moment!) or Inversion of Control containers?

Whichever option you choose, creation of objects can still be a chore, especially if the construction process is complicated or needs to abide by special rules. So that's where Creational patterns come from: they are common approaches related to the creation of objects.

Just in case you are rusty on your basic C++, or smart pointers in general, here's a brief recap of the way objects are created in C++:

- *Stack allocation* creates an object on the stack. The object will be cleaned up automatically at the end of the scope (you can make an artificial scope anywhere with a pair of curly braces). The object will call the destructor at the very end of the scope provided you assign this object to a variable; if you don't, the destructor will be called *immediately*. (This can ruin some implementations of the Memento design pattern, as we'll discover later.)

- *Heap allocation* using a raw pointer puts the object on the heap (a.k.a. the free store). Foo* foo = new Foo creates a new instance of Foo and leaves open the question of who is in charge of cleaning up the object. The GSL[1] owner<T> tries to introduce some idea of "ownership" of a raw pointer but doesn't involve any cleanup code – you still have to write it yourself.

- A *unique pointer* (unique_ptr) can take a heap-allocated pointer and manage it so that it's cleaned up automatically when there is no longer a reference to it. A unique pointer really is unique: you cannot make copies of it, and you cannot pass it into another function without losing control of the original.

- A *shared pointer* (shared_ptr) takes a heap-allocated pointer and manages it, but allows the sharing of this pointer around in code. The owned pointer is only cleaned up when there are no components holding on to the pointer.

- A *weak pointer* (weak_ptr) is a smart but non-owning pointer, holding a weak reference to an object managed by a shared_ptr. You need to convert it to a shared_ptr in order to be able to actually access the referenced object. One of its uses is to break circular references of shared_ptrs.

Most design patterns do not take a particular opinion on how an object should be created and returned, leaving it up to a developer. For example,

---

[1] The Guideline Support Library (https://github.com/Microsoft/GSL) is a set of functions and types that are suggested by the C++ Core Guidelines. This library includes many types, among them the owner<T> type used to indicate ownership of a pointer.

a factory might construct objects as unique_ptrs, but when you need a very large number of these objects, raw pointers might be a better choice.

Now, let us discuss how to return objects from functions. If you are returning anything bigger than a word-sized value, there are several ways of returning something from a function. The first, and most obvious, is

```
Foo make_foo(int n)
{
  return Foo{n};
}
```

It may appear to you that, in this example, a full copy of Foo is being made, thereby wasting valuable resources. But it isn't always so. Say you define Foo as

```
struct Foo
{
  Foo(int n) {}
  Foo(const Foo&) { cout << "COPY CONSTRUCTOR!!!\n"; }
};
```

You will find that the copy constructor may be called anywhere from zero to two times: the exact number of calls depends on the compiler. *Return value optimization* (RVO) is a compiler feature that specifically prevents those extra copies being made (since they don't really affect how the code behaves). In complex scenarios, however, you really cannot rely on RVO happening, but when it comes to choosing whether or not to optimize return values, I prefer to follow Knuth.[2]

---

[2] Donald Knuth, famous for his *The Art of Computer Programming* series of books, once wrote a paper which included the claim that "premature optimization is the root of all evil." C++ makes premature optimization very tempting, but you should resist the temptation until (a) you understand exactly what you're doing and (b) you actually experience a performance effect that requires optimization.

Another approach is, of course, to return a smart pointer such as a unique_ptr:

```
unique_ptr<Foo> make_foo(int n)
{
  return make_unique<Foo>(n);
}
```

This is very safe, but also opinionated: you've chosen the smart pointer for the user. What if they don't like smart pointers? What if they would prefer a shared_ptr instead? This means they would have to perform additional conversions and manipulations.

The third and final option is to use a raw pointer, perhaps in tandem with GSL's owner<T>. This way, you are not enforcing the cleanup of the allocated object, but you are sending a very clear message that it is the caller's responsibility:

```
owner<Foo*> make_foo(int n)
{
  return new Foo(n);
}
```

You can consider this approach as giving the user a *hint*: I'm returning a pointer and it's up to you to take care of the pointer from now on. Of course, now the caller of make_foo() needs to handle the pointer: either by correctly calling delete or by wrapping it in a unique_ptr or shared_ptr. Keep in mind that owner<T> says nothing about copying.

All of these options are equally valid, and it's difficult to say which option is best.

CHAPTER 2

Builder

The Builder pattern is concerned with the creation of *complicated* objects, that is, objects that cannot be built up in a single-line constructor call. These types of objects may themselves be composed of other objects and may involve less than obvious logic, necessitating a separate component specifically dedicated to object construction.

I suppose it's worth noting beforehand that, while I said the Builder is concerned with *complicated* objects, we'll be taking a look at a rather trivial example. This is done purely for the purposes of space optimization, so that the complexity of the domain logic doesn't interfere with the reader's ability to appreciate the actual implementation of the pattern.

Scenario

Let's imagine that we are building a component that renders web pages. To start with, we shall output a simple unordered list with two items containing the words *hello* and *world*. A very simplistic implementation might look as follows:

```
string words[] = { "hello", "world" };
ostringstream oss;
oss << "<ul>";
for (auto w : words)
```

© Dmitri Nesteruk 2022
D. Nesteruk, *Design Patterns in Modern C++20*,
https://doi.org/10.1007/978-1-4842-7295-4_2

```
oss << " <li>" << w << "</li>";
oss << "</ul>";
printf(oss.str().c_str());
```

This does in fact give us what we want, but the approach is not very flexible. How would we change this from a bulleted list to a numbered list? How can we add another item *after* the list has been created? Clearly, in this rigid scheme of ours, this is not possible.

We might, therefore, go the OOP route and define an HtmlElement class to store information about each tag:

```
struct HtmlElement
{
  string name, text;
  vector<HtmlElement> elements;

  HtmlElement() {}
  HtmlElement(const string& name, const string& text)
    : name(name), text(text) { }

  string str(int indent = 0) const
  {
    // pretty-print the contents
    // (implementation omitted)
  }
}
```

Armed with this approach, we can now create our list in a more sensible fashion:

```
string words[] = { "hello", "world" };
HtmlElement list{"ul", ""};
```

```
for (auto w : words)
  list.elements.emplace_back("li", w);
printf(list.str().c_str());
```

This works fine and gives us a more controllable, OOP-driven representation of a list of items. But the process of building up each HtmlElement is not very convenient, and we can improve it by implementing the Builder pattern.

Simple Builder

The Builder pattern simply tries to outsource the piecewise construction of an object into a separate class. Our first attempt might yield something like this:

```
struct HtmlBuilder
{
  HtmlElement root;

  HtmlBuilder(string root_name) { root.name = root_name; }

  void add_child(string child_name, string child_text)
  {
    root.elements.emplace_back(child_name, child_text);
  }

  string str() { return root.str(); }
};
```

This is a dedicated component for building up an HTML element. The add_child() method is intended to be used to add additional children to the current element, each child being a name-text pair. It can be used as follows:

```
HtmlBuilder builder{ "ul" };
builder.add_child("li", "hello");
builder.add_child("li", "world");
cout << builder.str() << endl;
```

You'll notice that, at the moment, the add_child() function is void-returning. There are many things we could use the return value for, but one of the most common uses of the return value is to help us build a fluent interface.

Fluent Builder

Let's change our definition of add_child() to the following:

```
HtmlBuilder& add_child(string child_name, string child_text)
{
  root.elements.emplace_back(child_name, child_text);
  return *this;
}
```

By returning a reference to the builder itself, the builder calls can now be chained. This is what's called a *fluent interface*:

```
HtmlBuilder builder{ "ul" };
builder.add_child("li", "hello")
       .add_child("li", "world");
cout << builder.str() << endl;
```

The choice of references or pointers is entirely up to you. If you want to chain calls with the -> operator, you can define add_child() like this:

```
HtmlBuilder* add_child(string child_name, string child_text)
{
  root.elements.emplace_back(child_name, child_text);
  return this;
}
```

And then use it like this:

```
HtmlBuilder builder{"ul"};
builder->add_child("li", "hello")
      ->add_child("li", "world");
cout << builder << endl;
```

Communicating Intent

We have a dedicated Builder implemented for an HTML element, but how will the users of our classes know how to use it? One idea is to simply *force* them to use the builder whenever they are constructing an object. Here's what you need to do:

```
struct HtmlElement
{
  string name;
  string text;
  vector<HtmlElement> elements;
  const size_t indent_size = 2;
```

```
  static unique_ptr<HtmlBuilder> create(const string& root_name)
  {
    return make_unique<HtmlBuilder>(root_name);
  }

protected: // hide all constructors
  HtmlElement() {}
  HtmlElement(const string& name, const string& text)
    : name{name}, text{text}
  {
  }
};
```

Our approach is two-pronged. First, we have hidden all constructors, so they are no longer available. We have, however, created a factory method (see Chapter 3, "Factories") for creating a builder right out of the HtmlElement. And it's a static method too. Here's how one would go about using it:

```
auto builder = HtmlElement::create("ul");
builder.add_child("li", "hello").add_child("li", "world");
cout << builder.str() << endl;
```

But let's not forget that our ultimate goal is to build an HtmlElement, not just a builder for it! So the icing on the cake can be an implementation of an implicit conversion operator that yield the final value:

```
struct HtmlBuilder
{
  operator HtmlElement() const { return root; }
  HtmlElement root;
  // other operations omitted
};
```

Anyways, the addition of the operator allows us to write the following:

```
HtmlElement e = HtmlElement::build("ul")
  .add_child("li", "hello")
  .add_child("li", "world");
cout << e.str() << endl;
```

Regrettably, there is no way of explicitly telling other users to use the API in this manner. Hopefully the restriction on constructors coupled with the presence of the static build() function gets the user to use the builder, but, in addition to the operator, it might make sense to also add a corresponding build() function to HtmlBuilder itself:

```
HtmlElement HtmlBuilder::build() const
{
  return root;
}
```

Groovy-Style Builder

This example is a minor digression from dedicated builders since there is really no builder in sight. It is simply an alternative means of object construction.

Programming languages such as Groovy, Kotlin, and others all try to show off how great they are at building DSLs by supporting syntactic constructs that make the process better. But why should C++ be any different? Thanks to initializer lists, we can effectively build an HTML-compatible DSL using ordinary classes.

First of all, we'll define an HTML tag:

```
struct Tag
{
  string name;
  string text;
  vector<Tag> children;
  vector<pair<string, string>> attributes;

  friend ostream& operator<<(ostream& os, const Tag& tag)
  {
    // implementation omitted
  }
};
```

So far, we have a Tag that can store its name, text, children (inner tags), and even HTML attributes. We also have some pretty-printing code that's too boring to show here.

Now we can give it a couple of protected constructors (because we don't want anyone to actually instantiate this directly). Our previous experiments have taught us that we have at least two cases:

- A tag initialized by name and text (e.g., a list item)

- A tag initialized by name and a collection of children

That second case is more interesting; we'll use a parameter of type vector:

```
struct Tag
{
  ...
protected:
```

```
Tag(const string& name, const string& text)
  : name{name}, text{text} {}

Tag(const string& name, const vector<Tag>& children)
  : name{name}, children{children} {}
};
```

Now we can inherit from this Tag class, but only for valid HTML tags (thereby constraining our DSL). Let's define two tags: one for a paragraph and another for an image:

```
struct P : Tag
{
  explicit P(const string& text)
    : Tag{"p", text} {}

  P(initializer_list<Tag> children)
    : Tag("p", children) {}

};

struct IMG : Tag
{
  explicit IMG(const string& url)
    : Tag{"img", ""}
  {
    attributes.emplace_back({"src", url});
  }
};
```

These constructors further constrain our API. A paragraph, according to these constructors, can only contain either text or a set of children. An image, on the other hand, can contain no other tag, but *must* have an attribute called img with the provided address.

And now, *the prestige* of this magic trick… thanks to uniform initialization and all the constructors we've spawned, we can write the following:

```
cout <<

  P {
    IMG { "http://pokemon.com/pikachu.png" }
  }

  << endl;
```

Isn't this great? We've built a mini-DSL for paragraphs and images, and this model can easily be extended to support other tags. And there's no add_child() call in sight!

Composite Builder

We are going to finish off the discussion of Builder with an example where multiple builders are used to build up a single object. Let's say we decide to record some information about a person:

```
class Person
{
  // address
  string street_address, post_code, city;

  // employment
  string company_name, position;
  int annual_income = 0;

  Person() {}
};
```

There are two aspects to Person: their address and employment information. What if we want to have separate builders for each – how can we provide the most convenient API? To do this, we'll construct a composite builder. This construction is not trivial, so pay attention – even though we want separate builders for job and address information, we'll spawn no less than *four* distinct classes. Figure 2-1 provides a visual illustration of what we intend to build.

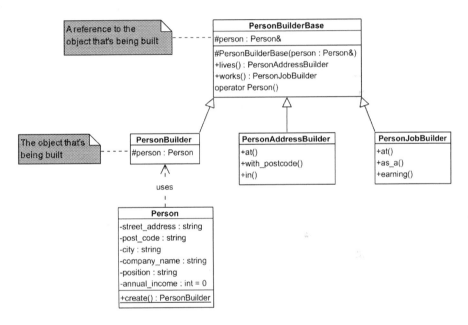

Figure 2-1. *Composite builder class diagram*

We'll call the first class PersonBuilderBase:

```
class PersonBuilderBase
{
protected:
  Person& person;
  explicit PersonBuilderBase(Person& person)
    : person{person} {}
```

```
public:
  operator Person()
  {
    return move(person);
  }

  // builder facets
  PersonAddressBuilder lives() const;
  PersonJobBuilder works() const;
};
```

This is *much* more complicated than our simple Builder earlier, so let's discuss each member in turn:

- person is a reference to the object that's being built. This may seem rather strange, but it's done deliberately for the sub-builders. Note that the physical storage of Person is not present in this class. This is critical! The root class only holds a reference, not the constructed object.

- The reference-assigning constructor is protected so that only the inheritors (PersonAddressBuilder and PersonJobBuilder) can use it.

- operator Person is a trick that we've done before. I'm making the assumption that Person has a properly defined move constructor – it's easy to generate one in an IDE.

- lives() and works() are functions returning builder facets: those sub-builders that initialize the address and employment information separately.

Now, the only thing that is missing from this base class is the actual object that's being constructed. Where is it? Well, it's actually stored in an inheritor that we'll call, ahem, `PersonBuilder`. That's the class that we expect people to actually use:

```
class PersonBuilder : public PersonBuilderBase
{
  Person p; // object being built
public:
  PersonBuilder() : PersonBuilderBase{p} {}
};
```

So this is where the built-up object is actually built. This class isn't meant to be inherited: it's only meant as a utility that lets us initiate the process of setting up a builder.[1]

To find out why exactly we ended up with different public and protected constructors, let's take a look at the implementation of one of the sub-builders:

```
class PersonAddressBuilder : public PersonBuilderBase
{
  typedef PersonAddressBuilder self;
public:
  explicit PersonAddressBuilder(Person& person)
    : PersonBuilderBase{ person } {}

  self& at(string street_address)
  {
```

[1] This approach to separating the hierarchy into two separate base classes so as to avoid duplication of Person instances was suggested by @CodedByATool on GitHub – thanks for the idea!

```
    person.street_address = street_address;
    return *this;
  }

  self& with_postcode(string post_code) { ... }

  self& in(string city) { ... }
};
```

As you can see, PersonAddressBuilder provides a fluent interface for building up a person's address. Note that it actually *inherits* from PersonBuilderBase (meaning it has acquired the lives() and works() member functions) and calls the base constructor, passing a reference. It doesn't inherit from PersonBuilder though – if it did, we'd create far too many Person instances, and truth be told, we only really need one.

As you can guess, PersonJobBuilder is implemented in identical fashion. Both of the classes, as well as PersonBuilder, are declared as friend classes inside Person so as to be able to access its private members.

And now, the moment you've been waiting for: an example of these builders in action:

```
Person p = Person::create()
  .lives().at("123 London Road")
          .with_postcode("SW1 1GB")
          .in("London")
  .works().at("PragmaSoft")
          .as_a("Consultant")
          .earning(10e6);
```

Can you see what's happening here? We use the create() function to get ourselves a builder and use the lives() function to get us a PersonAddress Builder, but once we're done initializing the address information, we simply call works() and switch to using a PersonJobBuilder instead.

When we're done with the building process, we use the same trick as before to get the object being built up as a `Person`. Note that once this is done, the builder is unusable, since we moved the `Person` with `move()`.

Builder Parameter

As I have demonstrated, the only way to coerce the client to use a builder rather than constructing the object directly is to make the object's constructors inaccessible. There are situations, however, when you want to explicitly force the user to interact with the builder from the outset, possibly concealing even the object they're actually building.

For example, suppose you have an API for sending emails, where each email is described internally like this:

```
class Email {
public:
  string from, to, subject, body;
  // possibly other members here
};
```

Note that I said *internally* here – you have no desire to let the user interact with this class directly, perhaps because there is some additional service information stored in it. Some parts of the email (e.g., the `subject`) are optional, so the object doesn't have to be fully specified.

You decide to implement a fluent builder that people will use for constructing an `Email` behind the scenes. It may appear as follows:

```
class EmailBuilder{
  Email& email;
public:
  explicit EmailBuilder(Email &email) : email(email) {}
```

```
  EmailBuilder& from(string from)
  {
    email.from = from;
    return *this;
  }
  // other fluent members here
};
```

Now, to coerce the client to use only the builder for sending emails, you can implement a MailService as follows:

```
class MailService
{
  class Email { ... }; // keep it private
public:
  class EmailBuilder { ... };

  void send_email(function<void(EmailBuilder&)> builder)
  {
    Email email;
    EmailBuilder b{email};
    builder(b);
    send_email_impl(email);
  }
private:
  void send_email_impl(const Email& email)
  {
    // actually send the email
  }
};
```

As you can see, the send_email() method that clients are meant to use takes a function, not just a set of parameters or a prepackaged object. This function takes an EmailBuilder reference and then is expected to use this builder to construct the body of the message. Once that is done, we use the internal mechanics of MailService to process a fully initialized Email.

You'll notice there's a clever bit of subterfuge here: instead of storing a reference to an email internally, the builder gets that reference in the constructor argument. The reason why we implement it this way is so that EmailBuilder wouldn't have to expose an Email publicly anywhere in its API.

Here's what the use of this API looks like from the client's perspective:

```
MailService ms;
ms.send_email([&](auto& eb) {
  eb.from("foo@bar.com")
    .to("bar@baz.com")
    .subject("hello")
    .body("Hello, how are you?");
});
```

Long story short, the Builder Parameter approach forces the consumer of your API to use a builder, whether they like it or not. This function-based trick that we employ ensures that the client has a way of receiving an already-initialized builder object.

Builder Inheritance

One interesting problem that doesn't just affect the fluent Builder but any class with a fluent interface is the problem of inheritance. Is it possible (and realistic) for a fluent builder to inherit from another fluent builder? It is, but it's not easy.

Here is the problem. Suppose you start out with the following (very trivial) object that you want to build up:

```cpp
class Person
{
public:
  string name, position, date_of_birth;

  friend ostream& operator<<(ostream& os, const Person& obj)
  {
    return os
      << "name: " << obj.name
      << " position: " << obj.position
      << " date_of_birth: " << obj.date_of_birth;
  }
};
```

You make a base class Builder that facilitates the construction of Person objects:

```cpp
class PersonBuilder·
{
protected:
  Person person;
public:
  [[nodiscard]] Person build() const {
    return person;
  }
};
```

followed by a dedicated class for specifying the Person's name:

```cpp
class PersonInfoBuilder : public PersonBuilder
{
public:
  PersonInfoBuilder& called(const string& name)
  {
    person.name = name;
    return *this;
  }
};
```

This works, and there is absolutely no issue with it. But now, suppose we decide to subclass PersonInfoBuilder so as to also specify employment information. You might write something like this:

```cpp
class PersonJobBuilder : public PersonInfoBuilder
{
public:
  PersonJobBuilder& works_as(const string& position)
  {
    person.position = position;
    return *this;
  }
};
```

Sadly, we've now broken the fluent interface and rendered the entire set-up unusable:

```
PersonJobBuilder pb;
auto person =
  pb.called("Dmitri")
    .works_as("Programmer") // will not compile
    .build();
```

Why won't the preceding code compile? It's simple: `called()` returns *this, which is of type `PersonInfoBuilder&`; this simply doesn't have the `works_as()` method!

You might think the situation is hopeless, but it's not: you can design your fluent APIs with inheritance in mind, but it's going to be a bit tricky. Let's take a look at what's involved by redesigning the `PersonInfoBuilder` class. Here is its new incarnation:

```
template <typename TSelf>
class PersonInfoBuilder : public PersonBuilder
{
public:
  TSelf& called(const string& name)
  {
    person.name = name;
    return static_cast<TSelf&>(*this);
    // alternatively, *static_cast<TSelf*>(this)
  }
};
```

Well, this is classic CRTP. We introduce a new template argument, `TSelf`. We expect this argument to inherit from `PersonInfoBuilder<TSelf>`. This may seem odd, particularly because there isn't a single concept or static_assert in sight – sadly, in C++ self-referential checks like this are impossible because at a point where you need to perform those, you don't yet have a complete type.

The biggest problem in fluent interface inheritance is being able to return a *this reference that is typed to the class you're currently in, even if you are calling a fluent interface member of a base class. The only way to efficiently propagate this is by having a template parameter (the TSelf) that permeates the entire inheritance hierarchy.

To appreciate this, we need to look at PersonJobBuilder too:

```
template <typename TSelf>
class PersonJobBuilder :
  public PersonInfoBuilder<PersonJobBuilder<TSelf>>
{
public:
  TSelf& works_as(const string& position)
  {
    this->person.position = position;
    return static_cast<TSelf&>(*this);
  }
};
```

Look at the base class! It's not just an ordinary PersonInfoBuilder as before; instead, it's a PersonInfoBuilder<PersonJobBuilder<TSelf>>! So when we inherit from a PersonInfoBuilder, we set its TSelf to PersonJobBuilder so that all of its fluent interfaces return the correct type, not just the type of the owning class.

Does this make sense? If not, take your time and look through the source code once again. Here, let's test your understanding: suppose I introduce another member called date_of_birth and a corresponding PersonDateOfBirthBuilder, what class would it inherit from?

If you answered

```
PersonInfoBuilder<PersonJobBuilder<PersonBirthDateBuilder<SELF>>>
```

then you are wrong, but I cannot blame you for trying. Think about it: PersonJobBuilder is already a PersonInfoBuilder, so that information doesn't need to be restated explicitly as part of the inheritance type list. Instead, you would define the builder as follows:

```
template <typename TSelf>
class PersonBirthDateBuilder
  : public PersonJobBuilder<PersonBirthDateBuilder<TSelf>>
{
public:
  TSelf& born_on(const string& date_of_birth)
  {
    this->person.date_of_birth = date_of_birth;
    return static_cast<TSelf&>(*this);
  }
};
```

The final question is this: how do we actually construct such a builder, considering that it *always* takes a template argument? Well, I'm afraid you now need a new type, not just a variable. So, somewhere, you need to construct something like the following:

```
class MyBuilder : public PersonBirthDateBuilder<MyBuilder> {};
```

This is probably the most annoying implementation detail: the fact that you need to have a non-template inheritor of a recursive template type in order to use it.

That said, putting everything together, you can now use the builder, leveraging all methods in the inheritance chain:

```
MyBuilder mb;
auto me =
  mb.called("Dmitri")
    .works_as("Programmer")
    .born_on("01/01/1980")
    .build();
cout << me;
// name: Dmitri position: Programmer date_of_birth: 01/01/1980
```

Summary

The goal of the Builder pattern is to define a component dedicated entirely to piecewise construction of a complicated object or set of objects. We have observed the following key characteristics of a Builder:

- Builders can have a fluent interface that is usable for complicated construction using a single invocation chain. To support this, builder functions should return this or *this.

- To force the user of the API to use a Builder, we can make the target object's constructors inaccessible and then define a static create() function that returns the builder.

- A builder can be coerced to the object itself by defining the appropriate operator.

- Groovy-style builders are possible in C++ thanks to uniform initializer syntax. This approach is very general and allows for the creation of diverse DSLs.

- A single builder interface can expose multiple sub-builders. Through clever use of inheritance and fluent interfaces, one can jump from one builder to another with ease.

Just to reiterate something that I've already mentioned, the use of the Builder pattern makes sense when the construction of the object is a *nontrivial* process. Simple objects that are unambiguously constructed from a limited number of sensibly named constructor parameters should probably use a constructor (or dependency injection) without necessitating a Builder as such.

CHAPTER 3

Factories

I had a problem and tried to use Java, now I have a ProblemFactory.

—Old Java joke

This chapter covers two GoF patterns at the same time: *factory method* and *abstract factory*. These patterns are closely related, so we'll discuss them together.

Scenario

We're going to consider a very simple model of building construction where a building is made of walls. A wall is a structure consisting of

- Start and end 2D points defining the two bottom points of the wall

- The wall *elevation*, that is, the height or the z coordinate of the bottom of the wall relative to some baseline

- The height of the wall

© Dmitri Nesteruk 2022
D. Nesteruk, *Design Patterns in Modern C++20,*
https://doi.org/10.1007/978-1-4842-7295-4_3

We can model this wall as

```cpp
class Wall
{
  Point2D start, end;
  int elevation, height;
public:
  Wall(Point2D start, Point2D end, int elevation, int height)
    : start{start}, end{end}, elevation{elevation}, height
    {height} { }
};
```

To make things a bit more complicated, we can expand this "thin" wall into a SolidWall that has information about the width of the wall (i.e., how thick it is) and what material it's made of:

```cpp
enum class Material
{
  brick,
  aerated_concrete,
  drywall
};

class SolidWall : public Wall
{
  int width;
  Material material;
public:
  SolidWall(Point2D start, Point2D end, int elevation,
    int height, int width, Material material)
    : Wall{start, end, elevation, height},
      width{width}, material{material} {}
};
```

At the moment, both classes have public constructors that can be called directly. However, in the case of `SolidWall`, let's imagine that we decide to introduce a few real-world constraints. For example, let's assume that

- Aerated concrete cannot be used for underground construction.

- Minimum brick wall width is 120mm.[1]

These constraints need to be incorporated into the construction of a `SolidWall`, but how? Since a constructor cannot return an arbitrary data type, a reasonable way to validate input is to throw exceptions:

```
SolidWall::SolidWall(const Point2D start, const Point2D end,
                     const int elevation,
                     const int height, const int width,
                     const Material material)
  : Wall{start, end, elevation, height},
    width{width}, material{material}
{
  if (elevation < 0 && material == Material::aerated_concrete)
    throw invalid_argument("elevation");

  if (width < 120 && material == Material::brick)
    throw invalid_argument("width");
}
```

There are many reasons why this might not be the best approach. First, one might argue that validation is a separate concern, and if the number and complexity of these checks increases, it feels wrong to include them in the constructor. But the real problem is that we're constrained

---

[1] This assumes that the standard brick size is 250×120×65mm. Standard brick dimensions vary from country to country.

to exceptions: we cannot, for example, simply refuse to construct a
SolidWall, returning some error code or null value.

In truth, if we're using block materials, we cannot use arbitrary walls.
The problem is that factories which make those blocks produce a few
fixed sizes that are most useful to builders. As a consequence of this, we
ourselves can only build specific types of walls.

Factory Method

Let's remove the validation code from the constructor for now and make
the constructor protected. We can now add a pair of static methods that
would construct a SolidWall with predefined sizes and materials:

```
class SolidWall : public Wall
{
  int width;
  Material material;
protected:
  SolidWall(const Point2D start, const Point2D end,
    const int elevation,
    const int height, const int width, const Material material);
public:
  static SolidWall create_main(Point2D start, Point2D end,
    int elevation, int height)
  {
    return SolidWall{start, end, elevation, height,
                     375, Material::aerated_concrete};
  }

  static unique_ptr<SolidWall> create_partition(Point2D start,
    Point2D end,
    int elevation, int height)
```

```
{
  return make_unique<SolidWall>(start, end, elevation,
    height, 120, Material::brick);
}
};
```

The manner in which an object is returned is entirely up to you. In the case of the construction of a main wall (375mm aerated concrete), we return the constructed object by value. In the second method, used to create partition walls, we use 120mm bricks and return the wall as a `unique_ptr`.

Both of the static methods are called *factory methods*. They coerce the user to create these specific types of walls rather than just any arbitrary type. A factory method would be used thus:

```
const auto main_wall = SolidWall::create_main({0,0}, {0,3000},
2700, 3000);
cout << main_wall << "\n";
// start: (0,0) end: (0,3000) elevation: 2700 height: 3000
// width: 375 material: aerated concrete
```

The choice to make the constructor protected is optional: you can keep both some predefined factory methods *and* have a public fully-initializing constructor if this model suits you. Alternatively, you can make it private if you don't plan on inheriting from this class.

Factory

You'll notice that in the factory methods, we got rid of validation. Some of it is no longer necessary, but we still cannot allow aerated concrete underground. We could, for example, redefine the factory method like this:

```
static shared_ptr<SolidWall> create_main(Point2D start,
  Point2D end, int elevation, int height)
{
  if (elevation < 0) return {};

  return make_shared<SolidWall>(start, end, elevation, height,
    375, Material::aerated_concrete);
}
```

Note that the design choice here is to use a shared_ptr and return a default value if the validation fails. This allows us to have a factory method that can say *no* if some parameters are not satisfied:

```
// this will fail
const auto also_main_wall =
  SolidWall::create_main({0,0}, {10000,0}, -2000, 3000);
if (!also_main_wall)
  cout << "Main wall not created\n";
```

But imagine that interior walls cannot be created if they intersect other interior walls. How would you implement this? You need to track every partition wall created so far, but where would you store this information? It doesn't make sense to store it in SolidWall – particularly if similar mechanisms also require polymorphic interactions.

In order to solve this, we introduce a *factory*: a separate class whose responsibility is to construct objects of a particular type. We can define WallFactory as

```cpp
class WallFactory
{
  static vector<weak_ptr<Wall>> walls;
public:
  static shared_ptr<SolidWall> create_main(Point2D start,
    Point2D end, int elevation, int height)
  {
    // as before
  }

  static shared_ptr<SolidWall> create_partition(Point2D start,
    Point2D end,
    int elevation, int height)
  {
    const auto this_wall =
      new SolidWall{start, end, elevation, height, 120,
      Material::brick};

    // ensure we don't intersect other walls
    for (const auto wall: walls)
    {
      if (auto p = wall.lock())
      {
        if (this_wall->intersects(*p))
        {
          delete this_wall;
          return {};
        }
      }
    }
```

```
    shared_ptr<SolidWall> ptr(this_wall);
    walls.push_back(ptr);
    return ptr;
  }
};
```

This code keeps every constructed wall inside a vector<weak_ptr<Wall>>. We first of all construct a SolidWall the old-fashioned way, that is, using new, and then check whether or not it intersects any of the existing walls. If it does, we delete it and return a default pointer. Otherwise, we wrap the raw pointer with a shared_ptr, store it as a weak_ptr, and then return it.

There are a few important things that need to be noted here:

- If we want to keep the SolidWall constructor private or protected, the SolidWall class must declare friend class WallFactory, which is a clear violation of OCP.

- Even if we had declared the friend class, we would still not be able to use make_shared. This isn't an issue here (since we're keeping a weak_ptr), but in general, this can also be a problem.

We can now start using the factory instead of the class it creates:

```
const auto partition = WallFactory::create_partition(
  {2000,0}, {2000,4000}, 0, 2700);
cout << *partition << "\n";
// start: (2000,0) end: (2000,4000) elevation: 0
// height: 2700 width: 120 material: brick
```

Factory Methods and Polymorphism

One advantage of factory methods, whether they belong to the constructed object or are held in separate factories, is that such a method can return polymorphic types. Of course, this throws out the idea of returning by value (since this would cause slicing), but we can return pointers – whether ordinary or smart.

Here's an example: suppose we decide to introduce an enum class that would specify that we need either a basic wall (remember, we have a Wall base class) or a SolidWall – either a main wall or partition wall.

```
enum class WallType
{
  basic,
  main,
  partition
};
```

We can define the following polymorphic factory method:

```
static shared_ptr<Wall> create_wall(WallType type, Point2D
start,
  Point2D end, int elevation, int height)
{
  switch (type)
  {
  case WallType::main:
    return make_shared<SolidWall>(start, end, elevation, height,
      375, Material::aerated_concrete);
  case WallType::partition:
    return make_shared<SolidWall>(start, end, elevation, height,
      120, Material::brick);
  case WallType::basic:
```

```
//return make_shared<Wall>(start, end, elevation, height);
return shared_ptr<Wall>{new Wall(start, end, elevation,
height)};
}
return {};
}
```

I have once again removed any trace of validation from this method to simplify things. As you can see, the return type here is shared_ptr<Wall>, but in some cases, we construct a shared_ptr<SolidWall> instead. Here is how you would use this method:

```
const auto also_partition =
  WallFactory::create_wall(WallType::partition, {0,0},
  {5000,0}, 0, 4200);
if (also_partition)
  cout << *dynamic_pointer_cast<SolidWall>(also_partition) << "\n";
```

When working with polymorphic factory methods, you need to be aware of the obvious things: anything that's not virtual will be taken from the base class. For example, if both Wall and SolidWall define ostream& operator<<, without a dynamic_pointer_cast you'll only be seeing the output for the Wall portion of the class.

Nested Factory

Up until now, our migration path from constructor to factory has been as follows:

- We made the object's constructor protected.

- We declared the factory to be a friend of the object being constructed. If you have a hierarchy of types, this operation needs to be done for every single element in the hierarchy – not very convenient!

- We created the objects inside factory methods and
  returned them as shared_ptrs. Notice that inside the
  factory methods, we don't call make_shared – because,
  sadly, we cannot.

The biggest issue with all of this is the entanglement between the
object and the factory which creates it. If the factory is constructed *after*
the object, and we control the source code, the inclusion of the friend
declaration is an obvious violation of OCP. But if the factory is being
made for an object you do not even own, making it a friend isn't even a
possibility.

There is a third option which must also be considered if you are
prepared to entangle the factory and the object right from the start. This
approach is to create a *nested* (inner) factory, that is, the approach where
the factory is defined within the object itself:

```
class Wall
{
  // other members as before
private:
  class BasicWallFactory
  {
    BasicWallFactory() = default;
  public:
    shared_ptr<Wall> create(const Point2D start,
      const Point2D end,
      const int elevation, const int height)
    {
      Wall* wall = new Wall(start, end, elevation, height);
      return shared_ptr<Wall>(wall);
    }
  };
```

```
public:
  static BasicWallFactory factory;
};
```

There are a few things to note about the `BasicWallFactory` class:

- The factory itself is in a private block and has a private constructor. This is done so nobody tries to initialize it directly.

- The factory method is not static, unlike the previous examples we've seen.

- The `Wall` class exposes the factory as a static field.[2]

This allows us to use the factory as follows:

```
auto basic = Wall::factory.create({0,0}, {5000,0}, 0, 3000);
cout << *basic << "\n";
```

An entirely different set of choices would have to be made if you alter the design presented here. For example, if you were to put the `BasicWallFactory` class into a public block instead, you wouldn't need to put a `friend` declaration into the factory. Or, for example, if you find the use of both `::` and `.` annoying, you can make the factory's methods static too and call the factory method as `Wall::factory::create()`.

Abstract Factory

So far, we've been looking at the construction of a single object. Sometimes, you might be involved in the creation of families of objects. This is actually a pretty *rare* case, so unlike factory method and just plain

---

[2] In this case, as in many others, I tend to omit the code that initializes static variables with default values.

old Factory pattern, abstract factory is a pattern that only shows up in complicated systems. We need to talk about it, anyway, primarily for historical reasons.

Here's a simple scenario: suppose you are working at a café that serves tea and coffee. These two hot beverages are made through entirely different apparatus that we can both model as factories, of sorts. Tea and coffee can actually be served both hot or cold, but let's focus on the hot variety. First of all, we can define what a HotDrink is:

```cpp
struct HotDrink
{
  virtual void prepare(int volume) = 0;
};
```

The function prepare is what we would call to prepare a hot drink with a specific volume. For example, for a type Tea, it would be implemented as

```cpp
struct Tea : HotDrink
{
  void prepare(int volume) override
  {
    cout << "Take tea bag, boil water, pour " << volume
      << "ml, add some lemon" << endl;
  }
};
```

and similarly for the Coffee type. At this point, we could write a hypothetical make_drink() function that would take the *name* of a drink and make that drink. Given a discrete set of cases, it can look rather tedious:

```cpp
unique_ptr<HotDrink> make_drink(string type)
{
  unique_ptr<HotDrink> drink;
  if (type == "tea")
```

```
  {
    drink = make_unique<Tea>();
    drink->prepare(200);
  }
  else
  {
    drink = make_unique<Coffee>();
    drink->prepare(50);
  }
  return drink;
}
```

Now, remember, different drinks are made by different machinery. In our case, we're interested in hot drinks, which we'll model through the aptly named HotDrinkFactory:

```
class HotDrinkFactory
{
public:
  virtual unique_ptr<HotDrink> make() const = 0;
};
```

This type happens to be an *abstract factory*: it's a factory with a specific interface, but it's abstract, which means that even though it can feature as a function argument, for example, we would need concrete implementations to actually make the drinks. For example, in the case of making Coffee, we could write

```
class CoffeeFactory : public HotDrinkFactory
{
public:
  unique_ptr<HotDrink> make() const override
```

```
  {
    return make_unique<Coffee>();
  }
}
```

And the same goes for `TeaFactory` as before. Now, suppose we want to define a higher-level interface for making different drinks, hot or cold. We could make a type called `DrinkFactory` that would itself contain references to the various factories that are available:

```
class DrinkFactory
{
  map<string, unique_ptr<HotDrinkFactory>> hot_factories;
public:
  DrinkFactory()
  {
    hot_factories["coffee"] = make_unique<CoffeeFactory>();
    hot_factories["tea"] = make_unique<TeaFactory>();
  }

  unique_ptr<HotDrink> make_drink(const string& name)
  {
    auto drink = hot_factories[name]->make();
    drink->prepare(200); // oops!
    return drink;
  }
};
```

Here we made an assumption that we want drinks dispensed based on their name rather than some integer or enum member. We simply make a map of strings and the associated factories: the actual factory type is `HotDrinkFactory` (our abstract factory), and we store them through smart pointers rather than directly (makes sense, because we want to prevent object slicing).

Now, when someone wants a drink, we find the relevant factory (think of a coffee shop assistant walking to the right machine), create the beverage, prepare exactly the volume required (I've set it to a constant in the preceding listing; feel free to promote it to a parameter), and then return the relevant drink. That's all there is to it.

Functional Factory

One last thing I wanted to mention: when we use the term *factory*, we typically mean one of two things:

- A class that knows how to create objects

- A function that, when called, creates an object

The second option is not just a factory method in a classical sense. If someone passes an argument of type function<> (or just a basic function pointer) that returns a variable of type T, this is typically referred to as a Factory too and not a factory method. This may seem a little weird, but when you consider the idea that a method is synonymous with member function, it makes a bit more sense.

```
void construct(function<T()> f)
{
  T t = f();
  // use t somehow
}
```

Lucky for us, functions can be stored in variables, which means that instead of just storing a pointer to the factory (as we do in DrinkFactory), we can internalize the process of preparing exactly 200ml of a liquid. This is done by switching from factories to simply using function blocks, for example:

```
class DrinkWithVolumeFactory
{
  map<string, function<unique_ptr<HotDrink>()>> factories;
public:
  DrinkWithVolumeFactory()
  {
    factories["tea"] = [] {
      auto tea = make_unique<Tea>();
      tea->prepare(200);
      return tea;
    }; // similar for Coffee
  }
};
```

Of course, having taken this approach, we are now reduced to calling the stored factory directly, that is:

```
inline unique_ptr<HotDrink>
DrinkWithVolumeFactory::make_drink(const string& name)
{
  return factories[name]();
}
```

And this can then be used as before.

Object Tracking

Compared to calling a constructor, a factory is a little harder to use (being less obvious than a constructor), so it would be nice if there was a benefit associated with this trade-off. One benefit of using factories is you can track all the objects that have been constructed. We have already seen it before when we created a `WallFactory`.

The benefits are

- You know how many objects of a particular type have been created.

- You can perform modification of an entire *class* (in the mathematical sense) of objects, either modifying them or replacing them entirely.

- If you've given out a smart pointer, you can look at its reference count to determine the number of places where the object is used.

A Service Locator or an Inversion of Control container can adopt this approach. Such a container can construct objects as `shared_ptrs` but internally store `weak_ptrs` that can subsequently be not only inspected but, for example, replaced entirely at runtime by new objects.

As soon as you introduce this sort of construction, you have an ability to iterate over all the objects of type `MyClass` ever constructed. Remember, since these are `weak_ptrs`, at some point you'll need to clean up all the ones that are `expired()`.

This technique allows for a "runtime-compiled" approach where parts of the source code can be altered and recompiled while the application is running, and all existing instances of a particular object can be transparently replaced with updated instances without breaking the program and forcing us to recompile. This approach is, however, rather complicated, and a demonstration of such an implementation is beyond the scope of this book.

Summary

Let's recap the terminology:

- A *factory method* is a class member that is used for creating an object. It typically replaces a constructor.

- A *factory* is typically a separate class that knows how to construct objects, though, if you pass a function (as in `function` or similar) that constructs objects, this argument is also called a factory.

- An *abstract factory* is, as its name suggests, an abstract class that can be inherited by concrete classes that offer a family of types. Abstract factories are rare in the wild.

A factory has several critical advantages over a constructor call, namely:

- A factory can say *no*, meaning that instead of actually returning an object, it can return, for example, a default-initialized smart pointer, an `optional<T>` or a `nullptr`.

- A factory method can be polymorphic, so it can return a parent class/interface, or a pointer thereof. It can also support the return of different data types using other means, for example, via a `variant`.

- Naming is better and unconstrained, unlike the constructor name. You can call the factory methods whatever you want.

- A factory can implement caching and other storage optimizations; it is also a natural choice for approaches such as pooling or the Singleton pattern (more on this later).

- Factories can be used to encapsulate other concerns
  (as per Separation of Concerns) such as validation.

Factory is different from Builder in that, with a Factory, you typically create an object in one go, whereas with Builder, you construct the object piecewise by providing information in parts.

CHAPTER 4

Prototype

Think about something you use every day, like a car or a mobile phone. Chances are, it wasn't designed from scratch; instead, the manufacturer chose an *existing* design, made some improvements, made it visually distinctive from the old design (so people could show off), and started selling it, retiring the old product. It's a natural state of affairs, and in the software world, we get a similar situation: sometimes, instead of creating an entire object from scratch (the Factory and Builder patterns can help here), you want to take a preconstructed object and either use a copy of it (which is easy) or, alternatively, customize it a little.

And this leads us to the idea of having a Prototype: a model object that we can make copies of, customize those copies, and then use them. The challenge of the Prototype pattern is really the copying part; everything else is easy.

Object Construction

Most of object construction happens using, ahem, constructors. But if you've got an object configured already, why not simply *copy* that object instead of creating an identical one? This is particularly relevant if you've had to apply the Builder pattern to simplify piecewise object construction.

Let's consider a simple example, but one that clearly shows duplication:

```
Contact john{ "John Doe", Address{"123 East Dr", "London", 10 } };
Contact jane{ "Jane Doe", Address{"123 East Dr", "London", 11 } };
```

© Dmitri Nesteruk 2022
D. Nesteruk, *Design Patterns in Modern C++20*,
https://doi.org/10.1007/978-1-4842-7295-4_4

Both john and jane work in the same building, but in different offices. Many other people might work at 123 East Dr in London, so what we want to avoid is repeated initialization of the address. How can we do it?

The fact is the Prototype pattern is all about copying objects. And, of course, we do *not* have a universal way of actually copying an object, but there are options, and we'll choose some of them.

Ordinary Duplication

If what you are copying is a value, and the object you're copying stores everything through values, there's no problem. For example, if you define Contact and Address from the preceding example as

```
class Address
{
public:
  string street, city;
  int suite;
}
```

```
class Contact
{
public:
  string name;
  Address address;
}
```

there's absolutely no issue in making copies using the assignment = operator:

```
// here is the prototype:
Contact worker{"", Address{"123 East Dr", "London", 0}};
```

```
// make a copy of prototype and customize it
Contact john = worker;
john.name = "John Doe";
john.address.suite = 10;
```

In practice, this "by value" approach is quite a rare occurrence. In many cases, the inner Address object would be a pointer or a reference, for example:

```
class Contact
{
public:
  string name;
  Address *address; // pointer (reference, shared_ptr, etc.)
  ~Contact() { delete address; }
}
```

This throws a spanner in the works because now the line Contact jane = john copies the address *pointer*, so both john and jane and every other copy of the prototype share the same address, which we definitely do not want.

Duplication via Copy Construction

The simplest way of avoiding duplication is to ensure that copy constructors are defined on all the constituent parts (in this case, Contact and Address) that make up the object. For example, if we go with the idea of storing the address via an owned pointer, that is:

```
class Contact
{
public:
  string name;
```

```
  Address* address;
}
```

then you would need to create a copy constructor. There are actually two ways to do this, in our case. The head-on approach would look something like this:

```
Contact(const Contact& other)
  : name{other.name}
  //, address{ new Address{*other.address} }
{
  address = new Address(
    other.address->street,
    other.address->city,
    other.address->suite
  );
}
```

Unfortunately, this approach is not sufficiently generic. It will certainly work in this case (provided Address has a constructor that initializes all its members), but what if Address decides to fragment its street part into an object consisting of street name, house number, and additional information? Then you'll have that same copying problem again.

A sensible thing to do here would be to also define a copy constructor on Address. In our case, it's rather trivial:

```
Address(const string& street, const string& city,
  const int suite)
  : street{street}, city{city}, suite{suite} {}
```

Now we can rewrite the `Contact` constructor to reuse this copy constructor, that is:

```
Contact(const Contact& other)
  : name{other.name}
  , address{ new Address{*other.address} } {}
```

Mind you, if you use ReSharper's generator for **Copy and Move Operations**, it will also give you `operator=` which, in our case, would be defined as

```
Contact& operator=(const Contact& other)
{
  if (this == &other)
    return *this;
  name = other.name;
  address = other.address;
  return *this;
}
```

That's much better. Now, we can construct a prototype as before and then reuse it:

```
Contact worker{"", new Address{"123 East Dr", "London", 0}};
Contact john{worker}; // or: Contact john = worker;
john.name = "John";
john.suite = 10;
```

This approach works, and it works well. The only real issue here, and one that cannot be solved easily, is the amount of extra effort required to implement all those copy constructors. Granted, a tool like ReSharper makes quick work of most scenarios, but there are plenty of caveats. For example, what do you think would happen if I wrote

```
Contact john = worker;
```

and forgot to implement copy assignment for Address (but not for Contact)? That's right, the program would still compile. It's a little better with copy constructors because if you try to call one and it's missing, you get an error, whereas operator = is ubiquitous even if you haven't customized it to give it special behavior.

Here is another issue: suppose you start using something like a double pointer (e.g., void**)? Or a unique_ptr? Even with all their magic, tools like ReSharper and CLion are unlikely to generate correct code at this point, so rapid-firing code generation on these types might not be the best idea.

Virtual Constructor

The use of a copy constructor is rather limiting. One problem is that in order to make a deep copy of a variable, you need to know *exactly* what type that variable is. Consider a situation where an ExtendedAddress inherits from Address:

```
class ExtendedAddress : public Address
{
public:
  string country, postcode;

  ExtendedAddress(const string &street, const string &city,
    const int suite, const string &country,
    const string &postcode)
    : Address(street, city, suite)
    , country{country}, postcode{postcode} {}
};
```

Say you want to make a copy of a polymorphic variable:

```
ExtendedAddress ea = ...;
Address& a = ea;
// how do you deep-copy `a`?
```

This will be a problem because you don't really know what the most derived type of variable a actually is. That and the fact that copy constructors cannot be virtual leads us to seek other ways of creating copies of objects.

First of all, let us take the Address object and introduce a virtual clone() method. Our first attempt may look something like this:

```
virtual Address clone()
{
  return Address{street, city, suite};
}
```

Sadly, this will not work for purposes of inheritance. Remember, in the derived object, we want to return an ExtendedAddress, but our interface specifies the return type as just Address. We need polymorphism, which implies the use of pointers. Let's try again:

```
virtual Address* clone()
{
  return new Address{street, city, suite};
}
```

We can now do the same in the inheritor, but provide a covariant return type:

```
ExtendedAddress* clone() override {
  return new ExtendedAddress(street, city, suite,
                             country, postcode);
}
```

Now we can safely call clone() on polymorphic objects without worrying that some part of the object will be missing:

```
ExtendedAddress ea{"123 West Dr", "London", 123, "UK", "SW101EG"};
Address& a = ea; // upcast
auto cloned = a.clone();
```

And this works! The cloned variable is now a pointer to a deep-copied ExtendedAddress. Of course, its type is Address* so if you need those extra members, you'll either need a dynamic_cast or to call some virtual methods. For example, printing with cout << cloned will, unfortunately, only output data from the base class because the stream output operator is not virtual.

If, for some reason, you want copy constructors regardless, clone() could be simplified to

```
ExtendedAddress* clone() override {
  return new ExtendedAddress(*this);
}
```

All the work will then be done in the copy constructor.

One downside of this clone() approach is the compiler does not check that you've implemented clone() in every class in the hierarchy (and there is no way to enforce these checks). For example, if you forget to implement clone() inside ExtendedAddress, this demo will still compile and run just fine, but behind the scenes, the call to clone() will construct an Address rather than an ExtendedAddress.

Serialization

Designers of other programming languages have encountered this same problem of having to explicitly define copying operations on entire object graphs and quickly realized that a class needs to be "trivially serializable" –

that, by default, you should be able to take a class and write it to a string or a stream without having to anoint the class or its members with any extra annotations (well, maybe an attribute or two, at most).

Why is this relevant to the problem at hand? Because if you can serialize something to a file or to memory, you can then deserialize it, preserving all the information, including all the dependent objects. Isn't this convenient? Well...

Unlike other programming languages, regrettably, C++ does not offer us any free lunch when it comes to serialization. We cannot, for example, take a complicated object graph and serialize the entire graph to a file. Why not? In other programming languages, compiled binaries include not just executable code but plenty of metadata, and serialization is possible through a feature called *reflection* – which is so far unavailable in C++.

If we want serialization, then, just like with explicit copying operations, we need to implement it ourselves. Luckily, rather than fiddling bits and thinking of ways to serialize an `std::string`, we can use a ready-made library called Boost.Serialization to take care of some of this for us. Here's an example of how we would add serialization support to an `Address` type:

```cpp
class Address
{
public:
  string street;
  string city;
  int suite;
private:
  friend class boost::serialization::access;
  template<class Ar> void serialize(
    Ar& ar,
    const unsigned int version)
```

```
    {
      ar & street;
      ar & city;
      ar & suite;
    }
}
```

This may seem a bit backward, but the net result is that we've specified, using the & operator on all the parts of the Address that we would need to write to wherever we would be saving the object. Note that this is a member function for both saving and loading the data. It *is* possible to tell Boost to perform different operations on saving and loading, but this isn't particularly relevant to our prototyping needs.

Now, we also need to perform the same manipulation for the Contact type. Here we go:

```
class Contact
{
public:
  string name;
  Address* address = nullptr;
private:
  friend class boost::serialization::access;
  template<class Ar> void serialize(Ar& ar,
    const unsigned int version)
  {
    ar & name;
    ar & address; // note, no * here
  }
};
```

The structure of this serialize() function is more or less the same, but notice an interesting detail: instead of accessing the address as ar & *address, we still serialize it as ar & address, without dereferencing the pointer. Boost is smart enough to figure out what's going on and will serialize/deserialize things just fine even if address is set to nullptr.

So, if you want to implement the Prototype pattern this way, you need to implement serialize() on every single possible type that may appear in the object graph. But once you do, you can define a way of cloning an object via serialization/deserialization:

```
template <typename T> T clone(T obj)
{
  // 1. Serialize the object
  ostringstream oss;
  boost::archive::text_oarchive oa(oss);
  oa << obj;
  string s = oss.str();

  // 2. Deserialize it
  istringstream iss(oss.str());
  boost::archive::text_iarchive ia(iss);
  T result;
  ia >> result;

  return result;
}
```

And now, having a contact called john, you can simply write

```
Contact jane = clone(john);
jane.name = "Jane"; // and so on
```

and then customize jane to your heart's content. If you want, you can also put this clone() function into a Serializable<T> mixin class and then inherit from it in all objects that require cloning. This may be tedious if you have a large hierarchy of types, though.

Prototype Factory

If you have predefined objects that you want to replicate, where do you actually store them? A global variable? Perhaps. In fact, suppose our company has both main and auxiliary offices. We can declare global variables like this:

```
Contact main{ "", new Address{ "123 East Dr", "London", 0 } };
Contact aux{ "", new Address{ "123B East Dr", "London", 0 } };
```

We could, for example, stick these definitions into Contact.h so anyone using the Contact class would be able to take one of these global variables and make a copy of them. But a more sensible approach would be to have some sort of dedicated class that would store the prototypes and hand out customized copies of said prototypes on demand. This would give us additional flexibility. For example, we could make utility functions and hand out properly initialized unique_ptrs:

```
class EmployeeFactory
{
  static Contact main;
  static Contact aux;

  static unique_ptr<Contact> NewEmployee(
    string name, int suite, Contact& proto)
  {
    auto result = make_unique<Contact>(proto);
    result->name = name;
    result->address->suite = suite;
    return result;
  }
```

```
public:
  static unique_ptr<Contact> NewMainOfficeEmployee(
    string name, int suite)
  {
    return NewEmployee(name, suite, main);
  }
  static unique_ptr<Contact> NewAuxOfficeEmployee(
    string name, int suite)
  {
    return NewEmployee(name, suite, aux);
  }
};
```

This can now be used as follows:

```
auto john = EmployeeFactory::NewAuxOfficeEmployee("John Doe", 123);
auto jane = EmployeeFactory::NewMainOfficeEmployee("Jane Doe", 125);
```

Why use a factory? Well, consider the situation where we copy a prototype and then *forget* to customize it. It will have some blank strings and zeros where actual data should be. Using the approaches from our discussion of Factories, we can, for example, make all non-fully-initializing constructors private and declare EmployeeFactory as a `friend class`, and there you go – now the client has no way of getting a partially constructed Contact.

Summary

The Prototype design pattern embodies the notion of *deep* copying of objects so that, instead of doing full initialization each time, you can take a premade object, copy it, change it a little bit, and then use it independently of the original.

There are really two ways of implementing the Prototype pattern in C++, and both of them require manual manipulation. They are

- Writing code that correctly duplicates your object, that is, performs a deep copy. This can be done in a copy constructor/copy assignment operator or in a separate member function.

- Write code for the support of serialization/ deserialization and then use this mechanism to implement cloning as serialization immediately followed by deserialization. This has extra computational cost; its significance depends on how often you need to do the copying. The *only* advantage of this approach, compared to using, say, copy constructors, is that you get serialization for free.

Whichever approach you choose, some work will be required. Tools that support code generations (e.g., IDEs such as ReSharper and CLion) can help here if you decide to choose either of these two approaches.

Finally, don't forget that if you store all data by value, you don't really have a problem; operator = is all you need.

CHAPTER 5

Singleton

> *When discussing which patterns to drop, we found that we still love them all. (Not really – I'm in favor of dropping Singleton. Its use is almost always a design smell.)*
>
> —Erich Gamma

The Singleton is the most hated design pattern in the (rather limited) history of design patterns. Just stating that, however, doesn't mean you shouldn't use the singleton: a toilet brush is not the most pleasant device either, but sometimes it's simply necessary.

The Singleton design pattern grew out of a very simple idea that you should only have one instance of a particular component in your application. For example, a component that loads a database into memory and offers a read-only interface is a prime candidate for a Singleton since it really doesn't make sense to waste memory storing several identical datasets. In fact, your application might have constraints such that two or more instances of the database simply won't fit into memory or will result in such a lack of memory as to cause the program to malfunction.

© Dmitri Nesteruk 2022

D. Nesteruk, *Design Patterns in Modern C++20*,

https://doi.org/10.1007/978-1-4842-7295-4_5

Singleton As Global Object

The naïve approach to this problem is to simply agree that we are not going to instantiate this object more than once:

```
struct Database
{
  /**
   * \brief Please do not create more than one instance.
   */
  Database() {}
};
```

The problem with this approach, apart from the fact that your developer colleagues might simply ignore the advice, is that objects can be created in stealthy ways where the call to the constructor isn't immediately obvious. This can be anything – copy construction/assignment, a make_unique() call, or the use of an IoC container.

The most obvious idea that comes to mind is to offer a single, static global object:

```
static Database database{};
```

The trouble with global static objects is that their initialization order in different compilation units is undefined. This can lead to unpleasant effects, like a one global object referring to another when the latter hasn't yet been initialized. There's also the issue of discoverability: how does the client know that a global variable exists? Discovering classes is somewhat easier because **Go to Type** gives a much more reduced set than autocompletion after ::.

One way to mitigate this is to offer a global (or indeed, member) *function* which exposes the necessary object:

```
Database& get_database()
{
  static Database database;
  return database;
}
```

This function can be called to get a reference to the database. You should be aware, however, that thread safety for this is only guaranteed since C++11, and you should check whether your compiler is actually prepared to insert locks to prevent concurrent access while the static object is initializing.

Of course, it's very easy for this scenario to go bad: if Database decides to use some other, similarly exposed, singleton in its destructor, the program is likely to blow up. This raises more of a philosophical point: is it OK for singletons to refer to other singletons?

Classic Implementation

One aspect of the previous implementations that has been completely neglected is the prevention of the construction of additional objects. Having a global static Database doesn't really prevent anyone from making another instance.

We can easily turn life sour for those interested in making more than one instance of an object – simply put a static counter right in the constructor and throw if the value is ever incremented:

```
struct Database
{
  Database()
  {
```

```
    static int instance_count {0};
    if (++instance_count > 1)
      throw exception("Cannot make >1 database!");
  }
};
```

This is a particularly hostile approach to the problem: even though it prevents the creation of more than one instance by throwing an exception, it fails to *communicate* the fact that we don't want anyone calling the constructor more than once. Even if you adorn this with plenty of documentation, I guarantee there will still be some poor soul trying to call this more than once in some nondeterministic setting. Probably in production too!

The only way to prevent explicit construction of Database is to once again make its constructor private and introduce the aforementioned function as a *member* function to return the one and only instance:

```
struct Database
{
protected:
  Database() { /* do what you need to do */ }s
public:
  static Database& get()
  {
    // thread-safe since C++11
    static Database database;
    return database;
  }
  Database(Database const&) = delete;
  Database(Database&&) = delete;
  Database& operator=(Database const&) = delete;
  Database& operator=(Database &&) = delete;
};
```

Note how we completely removed any possibility of creating Database instances by hiding the constructor and deleting copy/move constructor/assignment operators. In pre-C++11 days, you would simply make the copy constructor/assignment private to achieve roughly the same result. As an alternative to doing this by hand, you might want to check out boost::noncopyable, a class that you can inherit that adds similar definitions in terms of hiding the members... except it doesn't affect move construction/assignment.

I will reiterate, once again, that if database depends on other static or global variables, using them in its destructor is not safe, as destruction order for these objects is not deterministic, and you might actually be calling objects that have already been destroyed.

Finally, in a particularly nasty trick, you can implement get() as a heap allocation (so that only the pointer, not the entire object, is static).

```
static Database& get() {
  static Database* database = new Database();
  return *database;
}
```

This implementation relies on the assumption that Database lives until the end of the program, and the use of a pointer instead of a reference ensures that a destructor, even if you make one (which, if you do, would have to be public), is never called. And no, this code doesn't cause a memory leak.

Thread Safety

As I've already mentioned, initialization of a singleton in the manner listed earlier is thread-safe since C++11, meaning that if two threads were to simultaneously call get(), we would never run into a situation where the database would be created twice.

Prior to C++11, you would construct the singleton using an approach called *double-checked locking*. A typical implementation would look like this:

```
struct Database
{
  // same members as before, but then...
  static Database& instance();
private:
  static boost::atomic<Database*> instance;
  static boost::mutex mtx;
};

Database& Database::instance()
{
  Database* db = instance.load(boost::memory_order_consume);
  if (!db)
  {
    boost::mutex::scoped_lock lock(mtx);
    db = instance.load(boost::memory_order_consume);
    if (!db)
    {
      db = new Database();
      instance.store(db, boost::memory_order_release);
    }
  }
}
```

Since this book is concerned with Modern C++, we won't dwell on this approach any further.

The Trouble with Singleton

Let's suppose that our database contains a list of capital cities and their populations:

```
Tokyo
33200000
New York
17800000
... etc
```

The interface that our singleton database is going to conform to is

```cpp
class Database
{
public:
  virtual int get_population(const string& name) = 0;
};
```

We have a single member function that gets us the population for a given city. Now, let us suppose that this interface is adopted by a concrete implementation called SingletonDatabase that implements the singleton the same way as we've done before:

```cpp
class SingletonDatabase : public Database
{
  SingletonDatabase() { /* read data from database */ }
  map<string, int> capitals;
public:
  SingletonDatabase(SingletonDatabase const&) = delete;
  void operator=(SingletonDatabase const&) = delete;

  static SingletonDatabase& get()
  {
    static SingletonDatabase db;
```

```
    return db;
  }

  int get_population(const string& name) override
  {
    return capitals[name];
  }
};
```

The constructor of the database reads the names and populations of various capitals from a text file and stores them in a map. The get_population() method is used as an accessor to get the population of a given city.

As we noted before, the real problem with singletons like the one we defined is their use in other components. Here's what I mean: suppose that, on the basis of the preceding, we build a component for calculating the sum total population of several different cities:

```
struct SingletonRecordFinder
{
  int total_population(vector<string> names)
  {
    int result = 0;
    for (auto& name : names)
      result += SingletonDatabase::get().get_population(name);
    return result;
  }
};
```

The trouble is that `SingletonRecordFinder` is now firmly dependent on `SingletonDatabase`. This presents an issue for testing: if we want to check that `SingletonRecordFinder` works correctly, we need to use data from the actual database, that is:

```
TEST(RecordFinderTests, SingletonTotalPopulationTest)
{
  SingletonRecordFinder rf;
  vector<string> names{ "Seoul", "Mexico City" };
  int tp = rf.total_population(names);
  EXPECT_EQ(17500000 + 17400000, tp);
}
```

This is a terrible unit test. It tries to read a live database (something that you typically don't want to do too often), but it's also very fragile, because it depends on the concrete values in the database. What if the population of Seoul changes (as a result of North Korea opening its borders, perhaps)? Then the test will break. But of course, many people run tests on continuous integration systems that are isolated from live databases, which makes the approach even more dubious.

This test is also bad for ideological reasons. Remember, we want a *unit* test where the unit we're testing is the `SingletonRecordFinder`. However, the test we wrote is not a unit test but an *integration* test because the record finder uses `SingletonDatabase`, so in effect we're testing both systems at the same time. Nothing wrong with that if an integration test is what you wanted, but we would really prefer to test the record finder in isolation.

So we know we don't want to use an actual database in a test. Can we replace the database with some dummy component that we can control from within our tests? Well, in our current design, this is impossible, and it is precisely this inflexibility that is the Singleton's downfall.

So, what can we do? Well, for one, we need to stop depending on `SingletonDatabase` explicitly. Since all we need is something implementing the Database interface, we can create a new ConfigurableRecordFinder that lets us configure where the data comes from:

```
struct ConfigurableRecordFinder
{
  explicit ConfigurableRecordFinder(Database& db)
    : db{db} {}

  int total_population(vector<string> names)
  {
    int result = 0;
    for (auto& name : names)
      result += db.get_population(name);
    return result;
  }

  Database& db;
};
```

We now use the db reference instead of using the singleton explicitly. This lets us make a dummy database specifically for testing the record finder:

```
class DummyDatabase : public Database
{
  map<string, int> capitals;
public:
  DummyDatabase()
  {
    capitals["alpha"] = 1;
    capitals["beta"] = 2;
    capitals["gamma"] = 3;
  }
```

```
  int get_population(const string& name) override {
    return capitals[name];
  }
};
```

And now, we can rewrite our unit test to take advantage of this `DummyDatabase`:

```
TEST(RecordFinderTests, DummyTotalPopulationTest)
{
  DummyDatabase db{};
  ConfigurableRecordFinder rf{ db };
  EXPECT_EQ(4, rf.total_population(
    vector<string>{"alpha", "gamma"}));
}
```

This test is more robust because if data changes in the actual database, we won't have to adjust our unit test values – the dummy data stays the same. Also, it opens interesting possibilities. We can now run tests against an empty database or, say, a database whose size is greater than the available RAM. You get the idea.

Per-Thread Singleton

We've mentioned thread safety in relation to the construction of the singleton, but what about thread safety with respect to a Singleton's own operations? It might be the case that instead of one singleton shared between all threads in an application, you need one singleton to exist per thread.

The construction of the per-thread singleton is identical to the one we've already seen before, except that the variable is now marked thread_local:

```
class PerThreadSingleton
{
  PerThreadSingleton()
  {
    id = this_thread::get_id();
  }
public:
  thread::id id;
  static PerThreadSingleton& get()
  {
    thread_local PerThreadSingleton instance;
    return instance;
  }
};
```

Our listing preserves the thread id for illustration purposes; you don't need to keep it if you don't want to. Now, to verify we're really getting one instance per thread, we can run something like

```
thread t1([]()
{
  cout << "t1: " << PerThreadSingleton::get().id << "\n";
});

thread t2([]()
{
  cout << "t2: " << PerThreadSingleton::get().id << "\n";
  cout << "t2 again: " << PerThreadSingleton::get().id << "\n";
});
```

```
t1.join();
t2.join();
```

This gives the output

```txt
t2: 22712
t1: 22708
t2 again: 22712
```

Thread-local singletons solve peculiar problems. For example, say, you've got a dependency graph similar to the following:

```
   needs        needs
A ------> B ------> C

   needs
A ------> C
```

Now, say, you spawn off 20 threads which all create an instance of A. The component A needs C twice: directly, and also indirectly through B. Now, if C is stateful and mutated in each thread, you cannot have one global CSingleton, but what you *can* do is create per-thread singletons. That way, an operation A will use the same instance of C both by itself and indirectly through B.

And, of course, an added benefit is that within a thread-local singleton you don't have to worry about thread safety, so you can use, say, a map instead of a concurrent_hash_map.

Ambient Context

Say, you're making building plans. You need to add walls to the ground floor of a house. These walls will have different positions, but the wall height for the entire floor will probably remain the same.

You can keep typing in the same value into dozens of method calls, but you don't want to. Nor do you want to declare a variable and pass that instead. You want to have some sort of global setting for wall height, the requirements being that

1. You can set a wall height, and it will be used as the default value.

2. But sometimes you want to do a few walls with a different height and then revert to the previous value.

3. And sometimes you want to specify the exact height via the API.

The height of the wall in this scenario is part of an *ambient context*: a set of states that are meaningful to a certain set of operations being undertaken at a particular point in time.

You can pass in an ambient context as an injected parameter into dozens of APIs, but this involves having lots of parameters and probably lots of delegate factories too! The only way to avoid this is to create a static construct addressable from within every point within the application.

Let's start defining the ambient context class:

```
class BuildingContext final
{
  int height{0};
  BuildingContext() = default;
```

As you can see, our ambient context class

- Is final: typically, it makes very little sense to support inheritance of ambient contexts.

- Has a private constructor, so it cannot be instantiated directly.

- Has a property for the height of the walls we plan to build. This property is read-only; we provide a get_height() accessor, but it cannot be modified from outside the class.

Moving on, we see some interesting members:

```
static stack<BuildingContext> stack;
// later initialized with
stack<BuildingContext> BuildingContext::stack(
  {BuildingContext{}});
```

Our ambient context statically stores several instances in a stack. Why? Take a look at Requirement 2 from our earlier list. Sometimes we want to build several walls (e.g., a chimney) at a height drastically different to the currently used height. How do we do this? We create a new state and push it on the stack. When we're done, we pop the stack and return to the old value.

Speaking of which, here is how one would do this:

```
class Token
{
public:
  ~Token()
  {
    if (stack.size() > 1) stack.pop();
  }
};
```

```
static Token with_height(int height)
{
  auto copy = current();
  copy.height = height;
  stack.push(copy);
  return Token{};
}
```

The with_height() method is just a helper piece of API. It creates a copy of the current context, alters it, and then puts the altered copy on the stack. The returned Token is a memento class only usable for its destructor. The idea is to define a scope and store the token in it (sadly, we cannot omit the variable declaration), causing the destructor to pop the value off the stack.

Now, given that we have a stack of states, the current ambient context is simply whatever exists on top of the stack. Notice our previously defined static constructor ensures that there's always at least one state there.

```
static BuildingContext current()
{
  return stack.top();
}
```

I will omit most of the plumbing required for this demo to work (see the source code for details), but I want to show you how you would handle Requirement 3 – an ability to override the ambient context value if needed. A Wall class with an optionally ambient height could be defined as

```
Wall::Wall(const Point2D &start, const Point2D &anEnd,
           optional<int> height = nullopt)
  : start{start}, end{anEnd}
{
  this->height = height.value_or(
    BuildingContext::current().get_height());
}
```

Thus, you can either provide your own value (in which case, height will be non-null) or let the class take it from the ambient context.

The use of the ambient context would appear as follows:

```
Building house;

// set default height to 3000
auto _ = BuildingContext::with_height(3000);

house.walls.emplace_back(Wall{{0,0}, {5000,0}});
house.walls.emplace_back(Wall{{0,0}, {0,4000}});

{ // temporarily set wall height to 3500
  auto _ = BuildingContext::with_height(3500);
  // now all added walls will use this height by default
  house.walls.emplace_back(Wall{{5000,0}, {7000,0}});
} // height reverts back to 3000 at end of scope

// uses wall height 3000 again
house.walls.emplace_back(Wall{{0,4000}, {3000,4000}});

// overrides to use wall height of 4000
house.walls.emplace_back(Wall{{0,4000}, {3000,4000}, 4000});
```

Having to declare auto _ variables is an unfortunate result of the fact that without variable declarations, the tokens returned by with_height() will be destroyed instantly, losing our height settings. Perhaps marking the method with [nodiscard] is a good idea.

An alternative way of dealing with the scoping issue is to accept a function in the body of with_height():

```
static void with_height(int height, function<void()> action)
{
  auto copy = current();
  copy.height = height;
  stack.push(copy);
```

```
  action();
  stack.pop();
}
```

With this approach, you can use an ambient context as follows:

```
BuildingContext::with_height(4000, [&]()
{
  house.walls.emplace_back(Wall{{0,0}, {5000,5000}});
});
```

Thus, within the scope of the lambda, the wall height will be set to 4000 and will revert to the previous setting at the end of the with_height() call. This approach obviates the Token class entirely. Also, this approach is not thread-safe; if you need concurrency, you need to lock the method (perhaps with a mutex) because otherwise two callers can push a value onto the stack and end up working with just one value instead of two distinct ones.

Singletons and Inversion of Control

The approach of explicitly making a component a singleton is distinctly invasive, and a decision to stop treating the class as a Singleton down the line will end up particularly costly. An alternative solution is to adopt a convention where, instead of directly enforcing the lifetime of a class, this function is outsourced to an Inversion of Control (IoC) container.

Here's what defining a singleton component looks like when using the Boost.DI dependency injection framework:

```
auto injector = di::make_injector(
  di::bind<IFoo>.to<Foo>.in(di::singleton),
  // other configuration steps here
);
```

In the preceding code, I use the letter I to indicate an interface type. Essentially, what the di::bind line says is that whenever we need a component that has a member of type IFoo, we initialize that component with a singleton instance of Foo.

Many developers believe that using a singleton in a DI container is the only socially acceptable use of a singleton. At least, with this approach, if you need to replace a singleton with something else, you can do it in one central place: the container configuration code. An added benefit is that you won't have to implement any singleton logic yourself, which prevents possible errors. Oh and did I mention that Boost.DI is thread-safe?

Monostate

Monostate is a variation on the Singleton pattern. It is a class that *behaves* like a singleton while appearing as an ordinary class.

```
class Printer
{
  static int id;
public:
  int get_id() const { return id; }
  void set_id(int value) { id = value; }
};
```

Can you see what's happening here? The class appears as an ordinary class with getters and setters, but they actually work on static data!

This might seem like a really neat trick: you let people instantiate Printer, but they all refer to the same data. However, how are users supposed to know this? A user will happily instantiate two printers, assign them different ids, and will be very surprised when both of them are identical!

The Monostate approach works to some degree and has a couple of advantages. For example, it is easy to inherit, it can leverage polymorphism, and its lifetime is reasonably well defined (but then again, you might not always wish it so). Its greatest advantage is that you can take an existing object that's already used throughout the system and patch it up to behave in a Monostate way, and provided your system works fine with the non-plurality of object instances, you've got yourself a Singleton-like implementation with no extra code needing to be rewritten.

The disadvantages are obvious too: it is an intrusive approach (converting an ordinary object to a Monostate is not easy), and its use of static members means it *always* takes up space, even when it's not needed. Ultimately, Monostate's greatest downfall is that it makes very optimistic assumptions that the class fields are always exposed through getters and setters. If they are being accessed directly, your refactoring is almost doomed to fail.[1]

Summary

Singletons aren't totally evil, but, when used carelessly, they'll mess up the testability and refactorability of your application. If you really must use a singleton, try avoiding using it directly (as in writing `SomeComponent.get().foo()`) and instead specify it as a dependency (e.g., a constructor argument) where all dependencies are satisfied from a single location in your application (e.g., an Inversion of Control container).

---

[1] To be fair, you *can* have your cake and eat it to, but you will need to use the non-standard `__declspec(property)` extension to do it.

PART II

Structural Patterns

As the name suggests, Structural patterns are all about setting up the structure of your application so as to improve SOLID conformance as well as general usability and refactorability of your code.

When it comes to determining the structure of an object, we can employ two fairly well-known methods:

- *Inheritance*: An object automagically acquires the non-private fields and functions of its base class or classes. To allow instantiation, the object must implement every pure virtual member from its parents; if it does not, it is abstract and cannot be created (but you can inherit from it).

- *Composition*: Generally implies that the child cannot exist without the parent. Think of an object having members of owner<T> type: when the object gets destroyed, they get destroyed with it.

- *Aggregation*: An object can contain another object, but that object can also exist independently. Think of an object having members of type T* or shared_ptr<T>.

Nowadays, both composition and aggregation are treated in an identical fashion. If you have a `Person` class with a field of type `Address`, you have a choice as to whether `Address` is an external type or a nested type. In either case, provided it's `public`, you can instantiate it as either `Address` or `Person::Address`, respectively.

I would argue that using the word *composition* when we really mean aggregation has become so commonplace that we may as well use them in interchangeable fashion. Here's some proof: when we talk about IoC containers, we speak of a *composition root*. But wait, doesn't the IoC container control the lifetime of each object individually? It does, and so we're using the word "composition" when we really mean "aggregation" here.

CHAPTER 6

Adapter

I used to travel quite a lot, and a travel adapter which lets me plug a European plug into a UK or US socket[1] is a very good analogy to what's going on with the Adapter pattern: we are given an interface, but we want a different one, and building an adapter over the interface is what gets us to where we want to be.

Scenario

Here's a trivial example: suppose you're working with a library that's great at drawing pixels. You, on the other hand, work with geometric objects – lines, rectangles, that sort of thing. You want to keep working with those objects but also need the rendering, so you need to *adapt* your geometry to pixel-based representation.

We begin our demo by defining two simple domain objects: a Point class that represents a two-dimensional point in Cartesian space (which can be assumed to correspond directly to the screen grid) and a Line segment defined by the start and end points.

---

[1] Just in case you're European like me and want to complain that everyone should be using European sockets: *no*, the UK design is technically better and safer, so if we did want just one standard, the UK one would be the one to go for.

© Dmitri Nesteruk 2022
D. Nesteruk, *Design Patterns in Modern C++20*,
https://doi.org/10.1007/978-1-4842-7295-4_6

```
struct Point
{
  int x, y;
};

struct Line
{
  Point start, end;
};
```

Let's now theorize about vector geometry. A typical vector object is likely to be defined by a collection of Line objects. Instead of inheriting from a vector<Line>, we can just define a pair of pure virtual iterator methods:

```
struct VectorObject
{
  virtual vector<Line>::iterator begin() = 0;
  virtual vector<Line>::iterator end() = 0;
};
```

So this way, if you want to define, say, a Rectangle, you can keep a bunch of lines in a vector<Line>-typed field and simply expose its endpoints:

```
struct VectorRectangle : VectorObject
{
  VectorRectangle(int x, int y, int width, int height)
  {
    lines.emplace_back(Line{ Point{x, y}, Point{x + width, y} });
    lines.emplace_back(Line{ Point{x + width, y}, Point{x +
    width, y + height} });
    lines.emplace_back(Line{ Point{x, y}, Point{x, y + height} });
```

```
  lines.emplace_back(Line{ Point{x,y + height}, Point{x +
  width, y + height} });
}

vector<Line>::iterator begin() override {
  return lines.begin();
}
vector<Line>::iterator end() override {
  return lines.end();
}
private:
  vector<Line> lines;
};
```

Now, here's the set-up. Suppose we want to draw lines on screen. Rectangles, even! Unfortunately, we cannot, because the only interface for drawing is literally this:

```
void DrawPoints(CPaintDC& dc, vector<Point>::iterator start,
  vector<Point>::iterator end)
{
  for (auto i = start; i != end; ++i)
    dc.SetPixel(i->x, i->y, 0);
}
```

I'm using the CPaintDC class from MFC (Microsoft Foundation Classes) here, specifically a SetPixel() method that, as you may have guessed, sets a particular pixel color (in our case, 0 = black) at particular coordinates.

The problem in our scenario is simple: we need to provide pixel coordinates to render graphics, but we only have vector objects.

Adapter

Say, we want to draw a couple of rectangles:

```
vector<shared_ptr<VectorObject>> vectorObjects{
  make_shared<VectorRectangle>(10,10,100,100),
  make_shared<VectorRectangle>(30,30,60,60)
}
```

In order to draw these objects, we need to convert every one of them from a series of lines into a rather large number of points. For this, we make a separate adapter class that will store the points and expose them as a pair of iterators.

```
struct LineToPointAdapter
{
  typedef vector<Point> Points;

  LineToPointAdapter(Line& line)
  {
    // TODO
  }

  virtual Points::iterator begin() { return points.begin(); }
  virtual Points::iterator end() { return points.end(); }
private:
  Points points;
};
```

The conversion from a line to a number of points happens right in the constructor, so the adapter is *eager:*[2] it does its work as soon as it is constructed. The actual code for the conversion is also rather simple:

---

[2] Could we have made the adapter lazy? Sure, we could just save the line locally (because it's a reference and we don't want it to go stale or change) and then,

```
LineToPointAdapter(Line& line)
{
  int left = min(line.start.x, line.end.x);
  int right = max(line.start.x, line.end.x);
  int top = min(line.start.y, line.end.y);
  int bottom = max(line.start.y, line.end.y);
  int dx = right - left;
  int dy = line.end.y - line.start.y;

  // we only support vertical or horizontal lines
  if (dx == 0)
  { // vertical
    for (int y = top; y <= bottom; ++y)
    {
      points.emplace_back(Point{ left,y });
    }
  }
  else if (dy == 0)
  { // horizontal
    for (int x = left; x <= right; ++x)
    {
      points.emplace_back(Point{ x, top });
    }
  }
}
```

The preceding code is trivial: we only handle perfectly vertical or horizontal lines and ignore everything else. Whether a line is horizontal or vertical, we construct a set of adjacent points that represent the lines in

---

whenever someone called begin(), perform initialization if it hasn't been done already. However, if we had *several* adapter members, this init check would have to be repeated in every single member.

terms of pixels. We avoid diagonal lines and the associated issues related to representing these lines smoothly (e.g., anti-aliasing).

We can now use this adapter to actually render some objects. We take the two rectangles defined earlier and simply render them like this:

```
for (const auto& obj : vectorObjects)
{
  for (const auto& line : *obj)
  {
    LineToPointAdapter lpo{ line };
    DrawPoints(dc, lpo.begin(), lpo.end());
  }
}
```

Here is what is happening:

- We take a vector of shared_ptr<GraphicObject> and go through every single one.

- We iterate directly on the dereferenced object (thus *obj), which results in the invocation of member begin()/end() functions.

- For every line that we iterate, we construct a separate LineToPointAdapter.

- And finally, we call DrawPoints(), which iterates the set of points the adapter has generated behind the scenes.

Adapter Temporaries

There's a major problem with our code, though: DrawPoints() gets called on literally every screen refresh that we might need, which means the same data for same line objects gets regenerated by the adapter, like a zillion times. What can we do about it?

Well, on the one hand, we can predefine all the points at application start-up, for example:

```
vector<Point> points;
for (auto& o : vectorObjects)
{
  for (auto& l : *o)
  {
    LineToPointAdapter lpo{ l };
    for (auto& p : lpo)
      points.push_back(p);
  }
}
```

and then the implementation of DrawPoints() simplifies to

```
DrawPoints(dc, points.begin(), points.end());
```

But let's suppose, for a moment, that the original set of vectorObjects can change. We don't know how they will change, but we do want to cache point data for all the unchanged ones and regenerate it for the modified ones.

First of all, to avoid regeneration, we need unique ways of identifying lines, which transitively means we need unique ways of identifying points. ReSharper's **Generate | Hash function** to the rescue:

```
struct Point
{
  int x, y;

  friend size_t hash_value(const Point& obj)
  {
    size_t seed = 0x725C686F;
    boost::hash_combine(seed, obj.x);
    boost::hash_combine(seed, obj.y);
```

```
    return seed;
  }
};

struct Line
{
  Point start, end;

  friend size_t hash_value(const Line& obj)
  {
    size_t seed = 0x719E6B16;
    boost::hash_combine(seed, obj.start);
    boost::hash_combine(seed, obj.end);
    return seed;
  }
};
```

I've opted for Boost's hash implementation. Now, we can build a new LineToPointCachingAdapter such that it caches the points and regenerates them only when necessary. The implementation is almost the same except for the following nuances.

First, the adapter now has a cache, which is map from the computed hash value to the set of points:

```
static map<size_t, Points> cache;
```

The type size_t here is precisely the type returned from Boost's hash functions. Now, when it comes to iterating the points generated, we yield them as follows:

```
virtual Points::iterator begin() { return cache[line_hash].
begin(); }
virtual Points::iterator end() { return cache[line_hash].end(); }
```

And here is the fun part of the algorithm: before generating the points, we check whether they've been generated already. If they have, we just exit; if they haven't, we generate them and add them to the cache:

```
LineToPointCachingAdapter(Line& line)
{
  static boost::hash<Line> hash;
  line_hash = hash(line); // note: line_hash is a field!
  if (cache.find(line_hash) != cache.end())
    return; // we already have it

  Points points;

  // same code as before

  cache[line_hash] = points;
}
```

Yay! Thanks to hash functions and caching, we've drastically cut down on the number of conversions being made. The only problem that remains is the removal of old points after they are no longer needed. This challenging problem is left as an exercise for the reader.

Bidirectional Converter

One problem when constructing user interfaces is being able to map UI control inputs to variables. For example, a text field that requires a numeric input will always, by design, store its internal state as a string, whereas what we might want to do is record the value as a number and, furthermore, perform some validation to ensure that a valid number was entered.

Quite often, what we want is a *bidirectional binding*: we want UI inputs to modify the underlying variable (e.g., a class field), but, at the same time, we want to make sure that if the variable was modified behind the scenes, the UI would be correspondingly updated.

We could define a stand-alone bidirectional converter by introducing a base class such as

```
template <typename TFrom, typename TTo> class Converter
{
public:
  virtual TTo Convert(const TFrom& from) = 0;
  virtual TFrom ConvertBack(const TTo& to) = 0;
};
```

Thus, you could explicitly define a converter between, say, an integer and a string like so:

```
class IntToStringConverter : Converter<int, string>
{
public:
  string Convert(const int &from) override
  {
    return to_string(from);
  }

  int ConvertBack(const string &to) override
  {
    int result;
    try {
      result = stoi(to);
    }
```

```
    catch (...)
    {
      return numeric_limits<int>::min();
    }
  }
};
```

Here is how you would use it:

```
IntToStringConverter converter;
cout << converter.Convert(123) << "\n"; // 123
cout << converter.ConvertBack("456") << "\n"; // 456
cout << converter.ConvertBack("xyz") << "\n"; // -2147483648
```

The last case is particularly interesting because it means that if the user enters something that doesn't parse as an `int`, we return the minimum numeric value instead. This is not the best approach in a real-world setting, since in most cases, you'd want to apply some validation beforehand and show an error message.

In the real world, we need to handle many concerns simultaneously: not only having an adapter to convert the values to and from but also validation, and for conversions to be done automatically on changes (via the Observer pattern).

Summary

Adapter is a very simple concept: it allows you to adapt the interface you have to the interface you need. The only real issue with adapters is that in the process of adaptation, you sometimes end up generating temporary data so as to satisfy some other interface. And when this happens, we turn to caching: ensuring that new data is only generated when necessary. Oh, and you'll need to do a bit more work if you want to clean up stale data when the cached objects have changed.

Another concern that we haven't really addressed is *laziness*: the current adapter implementation performs the conversion as soon as it is created. What if you only want the work to be done when the adapter is actually *used*? This is rather easy to do and is left as an exercise for the reader.

CHAPTER 7

Bridge

If you've been paying attention to the latest advances in C++ compilers (GCC, Clang, and MSVC in particular), you might have noticed that compilation speeds are improving. In particular, compilers are getting more and more *incremental*, so that instead of rebuilding the entire translation unit, the compiler can actually only rebuild the definitions that have changed and reuse the rest.

The reason I'm bringing up C++ compilation is because "one weird trick" has been consistently used by developers in an attempt to speed up compilation in the past.

I am, of course, talking about...

The Pimpl Idiom

Let me first explain the technical side of what happens in the Pimpl idiom. Suppose you decide to make a `Person` class that stores a person's name and allows them to print a greeting. Instead of defining `Person`'s members as you normally would, you proceed to define the class like so:

```
struct Person
{
  string name;
  void greet();

  Person();
  ~Person();
```

© Dmitri Nesteruk 2022
D. Nesteruk, *Design Patterns in Modern C++20*,
https://doi.org/10.1007/978-1-4842-7295-4_7

```
  class PersonImpl;
  PersonImpl *impl; // good place for gsl::owner<T>
};
```

Well, this is weird. Seems an awful lot of work for a simple class. Let's see... we have the name and the greet() function, but why bother with the constructor and destructor? And what's this class PersonImpl?

What you're looking at is a class that chooses to hide its implementation in yet another class, helpfully called PersonImpl. It is critical to note that this class is *not* defined in the header file, but rather resides in the .cpp file (Person.cpp, so Person and PersonImpl are colocated). Its definition is as simple as

```
struct Person::PersonImpl
{
  void greet(Person* p);
}
```

The original Person class forward-declares PersonImpl and proceeds to keep a pointer to it. It is precisely this pointer that gets initialized in Person's constructor and gets destroyed in the destructor; feel free to use smart pointers if it makes you feel better.

```
Person::Person()
  : impl(new PersonImpl) {}

Person::~Person() { delete impl; }
```

And now, we get to implement Person::greet() which, as you may have guessed, just passes control onto PersonImpl::greet():

```
void Person::greet()
{
  impl->greet(this);
}
```

```
void Person::PersonImpl::greet(Person* p)
{
  printf("hello %s", p->name.c_str());
}
```

So... that's the Pimpl idiom in a nutshell, so the only question is *why?* Why bother jumping through all the hoops, delegating greet() and passing this pointer? There are three advantages to this approach:

- A larger proportion of the class implementation is actually hidden. If your Person class required a rich API full of private/protected members, you'd be exposing all those details to your clients, even if they could never access those members due to private/protected access modifiers. With Pimpl, they can only be given the public interface.

- Modifying the data members of the hidden Impl class does not affect binary compatibility.

- The header file only needs to include the header files needed for the declaration, not the implementation. For example, if Person requires a private member of type vector<string>, you would be forced to #include both <vector> and <string> in the Person.h header (and this is transitive, so anyone using Person.h would be including them too). With the Pimpl idiom, this can be done in the .cpp file instead.

This allows us to preserve a clean, non-changing header file. A side effect of this is reduced compilation speed. And, what's important for us, the Pimpl idiom is actually a good illustration of the Bridge pattern: in our case, the pimpl *opaque pointer* (opaque is opposite of transparent, i.e., you have no idea what's behind it) acts as a bridge, gluing the members of a public interface with their underlying implementation that's hidden away in the .cpp file.

Bridge

The Pimpl idiom is a very specific illustration of the Bridge design pattern, so let's take a look at something more general. Suppose you have two classes (in the mathematical sense) of objects: geometric shapes and the renderers that can draw them on the screen.

Just as with our illustration of the Adapter pattern, we'll assume that rendering can happen in vector and raster form (though we won't be writing any actual drawing code here), and, in terms of shapes, let's restrict ourselves to just circles.

First of all, here is the Renderer base class:

```
struct Renderer
{
  virtual void render_circle(float x, float y, float radius) = 0;
};
```

We can construct vector and raster implementations easily; I'll just emulate actual rendering in the following with some code to write things to the console:

```
struct VectorRenderer : Renderer
{
  void render_circle(float x, float y, float radius) override
  {
    cout << "Rasterizing circle of radius " << radius << endl;
  }
};

struct RasterRenderer : Renderer
{
  void render_circle(float x, float y, float radius) override
  {
```

```
  cout << "Drawing a vector circle of radius " << radius << endl;
  }
};
```

The base class Shape shall keep a reference to the renderer; the shape will support self-rendering with the draw() member function and will also support the resize() operation:

```
struct Shape
{
protected:
  Renderer& renderer;
  Shape(Renderer& renderer) : renderer{ renderer } {}
public:
  virtual void draw() = 0;
  virtual void resize(float factor) = 0;
};
```

You'll notice that the Shape class rakes a reference to a Renderer. This happens to be the bridge that we build. We can now create an implementation of the Shape class, supplying additional information such as the position of the circle's center as well as the radius.

```
struct Circle : Shape
{
  float x, y, radius;

  Circle(Renderer& renderer, float x, float y, float radius)
    : Shape{renderer}, x{x}, y{y}, radius{radius} {}

  void draw() override
  {
    renderer.render_circle(x, y, radius);
  }
```

```
  void resize(float factor) override
  {
    radius *= factor;
  }
};
```

Okay, so this pattern is exposed rather quickly, and the interesting part is, of course, in draw(): that's where we use the bridge to connect the Circle (which has information about its location and size) to the process of rendering. And the exact thing which is the bridge here is a Renderer, for example:

```
RasterRenderer rr;
Circle raster_circle{ rr, 5,5,5 };
raster_circle.draw();
raster_circle.resize(2);
raster_circle.draw();
```

In this code, the bridge is the RasterRenderer: you make it and pass a reference into Circle, and from then on, calls to draw() would use this RasterRenderer as the bridge, drawing the circle. If you need to fine-tune the circle, you can resize() it, and the rendering will still work just fine, as the renderer doesn't know or care about the Circle and doesn't even take it as reference!

Figure 7-1 shows a class diagram of our Bridge implementation.

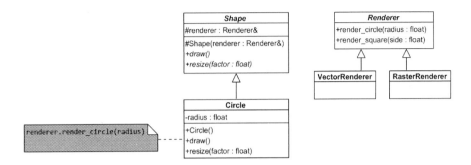

Figure 7-1. *Bridge class diagram*

Summary

The Bridge is a rather simple concept, serving as a connector or glue, connecting two pieces together. The use of abstraction (interfaces) allows components to interact with one another without really being aware of the concrete implementations.

That said, the participants of the Bridge pattern do need to be aware of each other's existence. Specifically, a Circle needs a reference to the Renderer and, conversely, the Renderer knows how to specifically draw circles (thus, the name of the draw_circle() member function). This can be contrasted with the Mediator pattern, which allows objects to communicate without being directly aware of each other.

CHAPTER 8

Composite

It's a fact of life that objects are quite often composed of other objects (or, in other words, they aggregate other objects). Remember, we agreed to equate aggregation and composition at the start of this part of the book.

There are very few ways for an object to advertise that it's composed of something. Fields, by themselves, do not constitute an interface unless you make virtual getters and setters. You *can* advertise classes as being composed of a collection of objects by implementing `begin()`/`end()` members, but keep in mind that this doesn't actually state a lot: after all, you can do *anything* you want in those methods. Similarly, you can try to advertise that you are a container of a *specific* type by doing an iterator typedef, but is anyone really going to check it?

An alternative to the use of the `begin()`/`end()` pair is the use of coroutines. These special functions' primary role is to allow the caller to suspend execution, but a byproduct is that they effectively expose generators that can yield a "resumable" sequence of values. We typically talk about generator *functions*, so if you wanted to define a generator *class*, you'd have to make a design choice about where the primary generator function would be. One choice would be to create a functor, that is:

```
class Values
{
public:
  generator<int> operator()()
  {
```

© Dmitri Nesteruk 2022
D. Nesteruk, *Design Patterns in Modern C++20*,
https://doi.org/10.1007/978-1-4842-7295-4_8

```
    co_yield 1;
    co_yield 2;
    co_yield 3;
  }
};
```

This allows us to invoke the functor in a common `for` loop and get the values thus:

```
Values v;
for (auto i : v())
  cout << i << ' '; // 1 2 3
```

On the other hand, this option does not aid discoverability in any way. Discoverability is often ignored entirely by C++ API creators, but I feel it is important to directly communicate this fact to the client. I *could* try to improvise a marker interface:

```
template <typename T> class Contains
{
  virtual generator<T> operator()() = 0;
};
```

But this is still a half-measure.

Another option for advertising being a container is... inheriting from a container. This is mostly fine: even though STL containers do not have virtual destructors, if *you* don't need anything in your destructor either, and you don't envisage people inheriting from *your* type, then everything is fine – go ahead and inherit from `vector`, nothing bad should happen.

So, back to the issue, what is the Composite pattern about? Essentially, we try to give single objects and groups of objects an identical interface. And sure, it's easy to just define an interface and implement it in both objects. But equally you can try leveraging duck typing mechanisms such as begin()/end() where applicable.[1] Duck typing, in general, is a *terrible idea* because it relies on secret knowledge instead of being explicitly defined in an interface somewhere. By the way, nothing prevents you from making an explicit interface with begin() and end(), but what is the iterator type?

Array-Backed Properties

The Composite design pattern is typically applied to entire classes, but before we get to that, I want to show you how it can be used on the scale of properties. By the term *property*, I am of course referring to the class' fields as well as the way those fields are exposed to the API consumer.

Imagine a computer game with creatures that have different numeric traits. Each creature can have a strength value, an agility value, and so on. So this is very easy to define:

```
class Creature
{
  int strength, agility, intelligence;
public:
  int get_strength() const
  {
    return strength;
  }

  void set_strength(int strength)
  {
```

---

[1] To be fair, the begin()/end() duopoly is excessive if all you care about is forward iteration until the end of the collection; you could take a cue from Swift and define an interface with a single member such as optional<T> next(). This way, you can just call next() until it gives you an empty value by writing something like while (auto item = foo.next()) { ... }.

```
    Creature::strength = strength;
  }
  // other getter and setters here
};
```

So far, so good. But now imagine you want to calculate some aggregate statistics on the creature. For example, you want to know the sum of its statistics, the average value across all statistics, as well as, say, the highest value. Since our data is fragmented into fields, we end up with the following implementation:

```
class Creature
{
  // other members here
  int sum() const {
    return strength + agility + intelligence;
  }

  double average() const {
    return sum() / 3.0;
  }

  int max() const {
    return ::max(::max(strength, agility), intelligence);
  }
};
```

This implementation is unpleasant for a number of reasons:

- When calculating the sum of all statistics, I could easily make a mistake and forget one of them.

- When calculating the average, I'm using a bona fide *magic number* 3.0 that corresponds to the number of fields that are used in the calculation.

- When calculating the maximum, I have to construct pairs of pairs of max() calls.

The code is terrible as is, but now imagine adding another property to the mix. This would require truly awful refactoring of sum(), average(), max(), and any other aggregate calculation. Can this be avoided? Well, it turns out it can.

The approach of using *array-backed properties* is as follows. First of all, we define enumeration members for all the required properties and then proceed to create an array of the appropriate size:

```
class Creature
{
  enum Abilities { str, agl, intl, count };
  array<int, count> abilities;
};
```

The preceding enum definition has an extra value called count which tells us how many elements we have in total. Note that we are using an enum, not an enum class, which makes the use of those members a little bit easier.

We can now define getters and setters for strength, agility, etc. being projected into our backing array, for example:

```
int get_strength() const { return abilities[str]; }
void set_strength(int value) { abilities[str] = value; }
// same for other properties
```

This is the kind of code that your IDE will *not* generate for you, but that's a small price to pay for the flexibility.

Now, here come the awesome parts: our calculations of sum(), average(), and max() become trivial because, in all of those cases, all we have to do is iterate an array:

```
int sum() const {
  return accumulate(abilities.begin(), abilities.end(), 0);
}

double average() const {
  return sum() / (double)count;
}

int max() const {
  return *max_element(abilities.begin(), abilities.end());
}
```

Isn't this great? Not only is the code a lot easier to write and maintain, but adding a new property to the class is as simple as adding a new enum member and a getter-setter pair; the aggregates need not change at all!

Grouping Graphic Objects

Think of an application such as PowerPoint where you can select several different objects and drag them as one. And yet, if you were to select a single object, you can grab that object too. Same goes for rendering: you can render an individual graphic object, or you can group several shapes together and they get drawn as one group.

The implementation of this approach is rather easy because it relies on just a single interface such as the following:

```
struct GraphicObject
{
  virtual void draw() = 0;
};
```

Now, from the name, you could be forgiven for thinking that a GraphicObject is always scalar, that is, it always represents a single item. However, think about it: several rectangles and circles grouped together represent a Composite graphic object (hence the name of the Composite design pattern). So just as I can define, say, a circle:

```cpp
struct Circle : GraphicObject
{
  void draw() override
  {
    cout << "Circle" << endl;
  }
};
```

In a similar vein, I can define a GraphicObject that is made up of several other graphic objects. Yes, the relationship can be infinitely recursive:

```cpp
struct Group : GraphicObject
{
  string name;

  explicit Group(const string& name)
    : name{name} {}

  void draw() override
  {
    cout << "Group " << name.c_str() << " contains:" << endl;
    for (auto&& o : objects)
      o->draw();
  }

  vector<GraphicObject*> objects;
};
```

Both a scalar `Circle` and any `Group` are drawable insofar as they both implement the `draw()` function. `Group` keeps a vector of pointers to other graphic objects (those can be `Group`s too!) and uses that vector for rendering itself.

Here's how this API can be used:

```
Group root("root");
Circle c1, c2;
root.objects.push_back(&c1);

Group subgroup("sub");
subgroup.objects.push_back(&c2);

root.objects.push_back(&subgroup);

root.draw();
```

The preceding code generates the following output:

```
Group root contains:
 - Circle
 - Group sub contains:
   - Circle
```

And this... is the simplest implementation of the Composite design pattern, albeit with a custom interface that we ourselves have defined. Now, how would this pattern look if we tried to adopt the approach of some of the other, more standardized ways of iterating objects?

Neural Networks

Machine learning is the hot new thing, and I hope it stays this way, or I'll have to update this paragraph. Part of machine learning is the use of artificial neural networks: software constructs which attempt to mimic the way neurons work in our brain.

The central element of neural networks is, of course, a *neuron*. A neuron can produce a (typically numeric) output value as a function of its inputs, and we can feed that value on to other connections in the network. We're going to concern ourselves with connections only, so we'll model the neuron thus:

```
struct Neuron
{
  vector<Neuron*> in, out;
  unsigned int id;

  Neuron()
  {
    static int id = 1;
    this->id = id++;
  }
};
```

I've thrown in the id field for identification. Now, what you probably want to do is connect one neuron to another, which can be done using

```
template<> void connect_to<Neuron>(Neuron& other)
{
  out.push_back(&other);
  other.in.push_back(this);
}
```

This function does fairly predictable things: it sets up connections between the current (this) neuron and some other one. So far so good.

Now, suppose we also want to create neuron *layers*. A layer is quite simply a specific number of neurons grouped together. Let us commit the cardinal sin of inheriting from `vector`:

```
struct NeuronLayer : vector<Neuron>
{
  NeuronLayer(int count)
  {
    while (count --> 0)
      emplace_back(Neuron{});
  }
};
```

Looks good, right? I've even thrown in the arrow operator `-->` for you to enjoy.[2] But now, we've got a bit of a problem.

The problem is this: we want to be able to have neurons connectable to neuron layers. Broadly speaking, we want this to work:

```
Neuron n1, n2;
NeuronLayer layer1, layer2;
n1.connect_to(n2);
n1.connect_to(layer1);
layer1.connect_to(n1);
layer1.connect_to(layer2);
```

As you can see, we've got four distinct cases to take care of:

1. Neuron connecting to another neuron

2. Neuron connecting to layer

---

[2] There is, of course, no `-->` operator; it's quite simply the postfix decrement `--` followed by greater than `>`. The effect, though, is exactly as the `-->` arrow suggests: in `while (count --> 0)`, we iterate until count reaches zero. You can do similar tricks with "operators" such as `<--`, `--->`, etc.

3.   Layer connecting to neuron

4.   Layer connecting to another layer

As you may have guessed, there's no way in Baator that we'll be making four overloads of the connect_to() member function. What if there were three distinct classes – would you realistically consider creating nine functions? I do not think so.

Instead, what we are going to do is slot in a base class – we can totally do that, thanks to multiple inheritance. So, how about the following?

```
template <typename Self>
struct SomeNeurons
{
  template <typename T> void connect_to(T& other)
  {
    for (Neuron& from : *static_cast<Self*>(this))
    {
      for (Neuron& to : other)
      {
        from.out.push_back(&to);
        to.in.push_back(&from);
      }
    }
  }
};
```

The implementation of connect_to() is definitely worth discussing. As you can see, it's a template member function that takes T and then proceeds to iterate *this and T&'s neurons pairwise, interconnecting each pair. But there is a caveat: we cannot just iterate *this, since this will give us a SomeNeurons& and what we're after is the actual type.

This is why we are forced to make SomeNeurons& come a template class where the template argument Self refers to the inheritor class. We then proceed to cast the this pointer to Self* before dereferencing it and iterating the contents. This implies that Neuron must inherit from SomeNeurons<Neuron> – a small price to pay for the convenience.

All that is left is to implement SomeNeurons::begin() and end() in both Neuron and NeuronLayer for the range-based for loops to actually work.

Since NeuronLayer inherits from vector<Neuron>, explicit implementation of the begin()/end() pairs is not required – it's automatically present there already. But the Neuron does need a way to iterate... itself, basically. It needs to yield itself as the only iterable element. This can be done as follows:

```
Neuron* begin() override { return this; }
Neuron* end() override { return this + 1; }
```

I'll give you a moment or two to appreciate the fiendishness of this design. It is precisely this piece of magic that makes SomeNeurons::connect_to() possible. In short, we've made a singular (scalar) object behave like an iterable collection of objects. This allows all of the following uses:

```
Neuron neuron, neuron2;
NeuronLayer layer, layer2;

neuron.connect_to(neuron2);
neuron.connect_to(layer);
layer.connect_to(neuron);
layer.connect_to(layer2);
```

Not to mention the fact that if you were to introduce a new container (say, some NeuronRing), all you would have to do is inherit from SomeNeurons<NeuronRing> and implement begin()/end() and the new class will be immediately connectable to both Neurons and NeuronLayers.

Shrink-Wrapping the Composite

We can construct a base class that would indicate that an object is a scalar:

```
template <typename T> class Scalar : public SomeNeurons<T>
{
public:
  T* begin() { return reinterpret_cast<T*>(this); }
  T* end() { return reinterpret_cast<T*>(this) + 1; }
};
```

Here we kill two birds with one stone: we inherit the connect_to() method from SomeNeurons and also implement the begin()/end() pair for a scalar value. We would thus define the Neuron class as

```
class Neuron : public Scalar<Neuron>
{
  // as before
}
```

And continue using it as before.

Conceptual Improvements

At the moment, the SomeNeuron class connects Neuron-containing things through duck typing. We could make a minor improvement by explicitly requiring that both of the connected types need to be iterable. To do so, we define a concept:

```
template <typename T> concept Iterable =
  requires(T& t)
  {
    t.begin();
    t.end();
```

```
} || requires (T& t)
{
  begin(t);
  end(t);
};
```

This concept is of limited use, however. It's very tempting to write something like

```
template <Iterable Self> // <-- a nightmare
struct SomeNeurons
{
  template <Iterable T> // <-- okay
  void connect_to(T& other)
  {
    // as before
  }
};
```

Declaring the connect_to() parameter as Iterable is fine. Declaring the type parameter Self to the class as Iterable is another matter entirely. From the outset, you could be forgiven for thinking that it should "just work," but it doesn't.

Consider the prior definition of the Scalar class. Since it inherits from SomeNeurons<T>, we need to constrain T to be iterable:

```
template <Iterable T> class Scalar : public SomeNeurons<T>
{
  // as before
};
```

However, this approach makes the definition of the Neuron class impossible. Remember, Neuron is defined as

```
struct Neuron : Scalar<Neuron>
```

Since Scalar explicitly requires that its type argument is iterable, we require that Neuron be iterable *in situ*, whereas it only becomes iterable due to inheritance from Scalar, and not before. Notice that even the order of inheritance does not matter here. For example, if you stopped Scalar inheriting from SomeNeurons and then defined Neuron as

```
struct Neuron : Scalar<Neuron>, SomeNeurons<Neuron>
```

it would *still* not compile despite the latter parent's requirements being fully satisfied by the former. What can I say, I guess concept-enabled CRTP is impossible.

Concepts and Global Operators

Now, I must admit, having a base class with a single function is a bit of a code smell. We can sort of tolerate it because C++ does not support extension methods (which would make short work of this), but let's take a look at an example where we would get rid of the SomeNeurons base class completely.

For my demo, I'm going to assume that we want to connect structures using operators instead of inherited methods. The -> operator is a natural choice, but, sadly, this operator can only be a *member* function, which would normally take us back to the idea of using a base class, where such a function could indeed be defined.

Being sly, however, we are going to introduce a different creature: operator --> which is, of course, just an amalgamation of the -- and > operators. The trick in the system is a two-step process:

1. Define a non-member operator -- which returns a special proxy class.

2. Give that proxy class the member > operator that is a
   * functional copy of connect_to() from earlier.

First, here's what the – operator would look like:

```
template <Iterable T> ConnectionProxy<T> operator--(T&& item, int)
{
  return ConnectionProxy<T>{item};
}
```

And here is the complete proxy:

```
template <Iterable T> class ConnectionProxy
{
  T& item;
public:
  explicit ConnectionProxy(T& item) : item{item} {}

  template <Iterable U> void operator>(U& other)
  {
    for (Neuron& from : item)
    {
      for (Neuron& to : other)
      {
        from.out.push_back(&to);
        to.in.push_back(&from);
      }
    }
  }
};
```

This allows us to connect two neurons, using very neat-looking code:

```
Neuron n1, n2;
n1-->n2;
```

Sadly, the discoverability of this approach is nonexistent: finding a single operator is bad enough, but finding a combination of two operators is a near-impossible challenge for a client. But hey, at least now you know how to define funky-looking operators.

Composite Specification

When I introduced the Open-Closed Principle, I gave a demo of the Specification pattern. The key aspects of the pattern were base types Filter and Specification that allowed us to use inheritance to build an extensible filtering framework that conformed to the OCP. Part of that implementation involved combinators – specifications what would combine several specifications together using AND or OR operators.

Both AndSpecification and OrSpecification made use of two operands (which we called first and second), but that restriction was completely arbitrary: in fact, we could have combined more than two elements together, and, furthermore, we could improve the OOP model with a reusable base class such as the following:

```
template <typename T> struct CompositeSpecification :
Specification<T>
{
protected:
  vector<unique_ptr<Specification<T>>> specs;

  template<typename... Specs> CompositeSpecification(Specs...
  specs)
  {
    this->specs.reserve(sizeof...(Specs));
    (this->specs.push_back(make_unique<Specs>(move(specs))),
    ...);
  }
};
```

The preceding code takes a number of specifications and stores them in a vector of owning Specification<T> pointers, thus dealing with issues of object slicing and polymorphic vectors. We've had to make use of variadics because an initializer_list<Specification<T>> would introduce slicing and, furthermore, had to use push_back() because of constness issues in the vector initializer.

With this approach, the AndSpecification combinator can now be implemented as

```cpp
template <typename T> struct AndSpecification :
CompositeSpecification<T>
{
  template<typename... Specs> AndSpecification(Specs... specs)
    : CompositeSpecification<T>{specs...} {}

  bool is_satisfied(T* item) const override
  {
    return all_of(this->specs.begin(), this->specs.end(),
      [=](const auto& s) { return s->is_satisfied(item); });
  }
};
```

This class simply repeats the constructor (I've omitted any hint of perfect forwarding for clarity) and provides an implementation of is_satisfied().

The intended use of the preceding class is as follows:

```cpp
auto spec = AndSpecification<Product>{green, large, cheap};
```

As you can see, all this combinator does is check that every single specification in specs is satisfied by the item. Similarly, if you wanted to implement an OrCombinator, you would use any_of() instead of all_of(). You could even make specifications that would support other, more complicated criteria. For example, you could make a composite such that the item is required to satisfy at most/at least/specifically a number of specifications contained within.

Summary

The Composite design pattern allows us to provide identical interfaces for individual objects and collections of objects. This can be done either through the explicit use of interface members or, alternatively, through *duck typing* – for example, range-based `for` loops don't require you to inherit anything and work on the basis of the typing having suitable-looking `begin()`/`end()` members.

It is precisely these `begin()`/`end()` members that allow a scalar type to masquerade as a "collection." It is also interesting to note that the nested `for` loops of our `connect_to()` function are able to connect the two constructs together despite them having *different* iterator types: `Neuron` returns a `Neuron*`, whereas `NeuronLayer` returns `vector<Neuron>::iterator` – these two are not quite the same thing. Ahh, the magic of templates!

Finally, I must admit that all of these jumps through hoops are necessary only if you want to have a *single member function*. If you are happy with calling a global function or if you are happy with having more than one `connect_to()` implementation, the base class `SomeNeurons` is unnecessary.

CHAPTER 9

Decorator

You're working with a class your colleague wrote, and you want to extend that class' functionality. How would you do it, without modifying the original code? Well, one approach is inheritance: you make a derived class, add the functionality you need, maybe even override something, and you're good to go.

Right, except this doesn't always work, and there are many reasons why. For example, you typically wouldn't want to inherit from, say, std::vector, due to its lack of a virtual destructor, or from an int (which is just impossible). But the most critical reason why inheritance doesn't work is the scenario where you need *several* enhancements, and you want to keep those enhancements separate because of the Single Responsibility Principle.

The Decorator pattern allows us to enhance existing types without either modifying the original types (and breaking the Open-Closed Principle) or causing an explosion of the number of derived types.

Scenario

Here is what I mean by *multiple* enhancements: suppose we have a class called Shape that represents graphical shapes (circle, square, and so on) and we need to give shapes color or a transparency value. We can make two inheritors called ColoredShape and TransparentShape, but then we also need to take into account the fact that someone will want a

© Dmitri Nesteruk 2022

D. Nesteruk, *Design Patterns in Modern C++20*,

https://doi.org/10.1007/978-1-4842-7295-4_9

ColoredTransparentShape. So we've generated three classes to support two enhancements; if we had three enhancements, we would need seven (seven!) distinct classes. Figure 9-1 presents a Venn diagram showing all the partitions generated by an intersection of three sets.

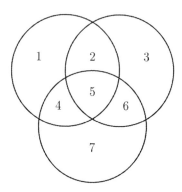

Figure 9-1. *Number of combinations of three sets. Intersections of larger numbers of sets become progressively more difficult to visualize*

And let's not forget that we actually want different shapes (Square, Circle, etc.) – what base class would those inherit from? With 3 enhancements and 2 distinct shapes, the number of classes would jump up to 14. Clearly, this is an unmanageable situation – even if you are using a tool for code generation!

Let's actually write some code for this. Suppose we define an abstract class called Shape:

```
struct Shape
{
  virtual string str() const = 0;
};
```

In this abstract class, str() is a virtual function we'll use to provide a textual representation of a particular shape, useful for our console-based demos.

We can now implement shapes such as Circle or Square that inherit from Shape:

```
struct Circle : Shape
{
  float radius;

  explicit Circle(const float radius)
    : radius{radius} {}

  void resize(float factor) { radius *= factor; }

  string str() const override
  {
    ostringstream oss;
    oss << "A circle of radius " << radius;
    return oss.str();
  }
}; // Square implementation omitted
```

We already know that ordinary inheritance alone does not offer us an efficient way to provide enhancements to shapes, so we must turn to composition – which is the mechanism that the Decorator pattern uses to enhance objects. There are actually two distinct approaches to this – and several other patterns – that we need to discuss:

- *Dynamic composition* allows you to compose something at runtime, typically by passing around references. It allows maximum flexibility since the composition can happen at runtime in response to, for example, the user's input.

- *Static composition* implies that the object and its enhancements are composed at compile time via the use of templates. This means the exact set of enhancements on an object needs to be known at the moment of compilation, since it cannot be modified later.

If this sounds a bit too cryptic, don't worry – we are going to implement the Decorator in both dynamic and static ways, so all will become clear very soon.

Dynamic Decorator

Suppose we want to enhance shapes with a bit of color. We use composition instead of inheritance to implement a ColoredShape that simply takes a reference to an already-constructed Shape and enhances it:

```cpp
struct ColoredShape : Shape
{
  Shape& shape;
  string color;

  ColoredShape(Shape& shape, const string& color)
    : shape{shape}, color{color} {}

  string str() const override
  {
    ostringstream oss;
    oss << shape.str() << " has the color " << color;
    return oss.str();
  }
};
```

As you can see, ColoredShape is itself a Shape (conforming to an interface that exposes str()), but it also keeps a reference to the shape it decorates – here it is an ordinary reference, but you're welcome to use a pointer, shared_ptr, or something else.

In addition to extra information about a shape's color, the ColoredShape can also have additional member functions such as

```
void ColoredShape::make_dark() {
  if (constexpr auto dark = "dark "; !color.starts_with(dark))
    color.insert(0, dark);
}
```

Well, that's some gratuitous use of constexpr, if-init, and C++20's starts_with() for you. Mind you, that function is about 20 years too late, as I'm sure you'll agree.

Here's how you would use this decorator:

```
Circle circle{0.5f};
ColoredShape redCircle{circle, "red"};
cout << redCircle.str();
// A circle of radius 0.5 has the color red

redCircle.make_dark();
cout << redCircle.str();
// A circle of radius 0.5 has the color dark red
```

If we now want another enhancement that adds transparency to shapes, this is also trivial:

```
struct TransparentShape : Shape
{
  Shape& shape;
  uint8_t transparency;

  TransparentShape(Shape& shape, const uint8_t transparency)
```

```
    : shape{shape}, transparency{transparency} {}
  string str() const override
  {
    ostringstream oss;
    oss << shape.str() << " has "
      << static_cast<float>(transparency) / 255.f*100.f
      << "% transparency";
    return oss.str();
  }
};
```

We now have an enhancement that takes a transparency value in the 0–255 range and reports it as a percentage value. We can now use the enhancement on its own:

```
Square square{3};
TransparentShape demiSquare{square, 85};
cout << demiSquare.str();
// A square with side 3 has 33.333% transparency
```

But the great thing about this dynamic approach is we can compose both ColoredShape and TransparentShape together to make a shape that has both color and transparency:

```
Circle c{23};
ColoredShape cs{c, "green"};
TransparentShape myCircle{cs, 64};
cout << myCircle.str();
// A circle of radius 23 has the color green has 25.098%
// transparency
```

If it's your intention to create such a structure in one line of code, you'd have to make adjustments to your code. At the moment, you cannot write something like

```
TransparentShape{ColoredShape{Circle{23}, "green"}, 64};
```

To get this to work, you would need to change the way you store references to the decorated object, by either using rvalue references, const references, or some other mechanism. It *will* work in MSVC due to its non-standard extension which allows to bind rvalue references to lvalues, but this is a non-portable solution.

Now, to be fair, one thing you also *can* do (though doesn't make much sense) is repeat the same decorator more than once. For example, it doesn't make sense to have a ColoredShape{ColoredShape{...}}, but it *will* work, giving somewhat conflicting results. And if you decide to fight against it with assertions or some OOP magic – well, you can do that, but I wonder how you will handle something like

```
ColoredShape{TransparentShape{ColoredShape{...}}}
```

This is much more challenging to detect, and even though it's possible, I would argue it's simply not worth checking. We need to assume *some* sanity on the part of the programmer.

Static Decorator

Did you notice that when setting up the scenario, we gave Circle a function called resize() that wasn't part of the Shape interface? As you may have guessed, since it's not part of Shape, you really cannot call it from a decorator. Here's what I mean:

```
Circle circle{3};
ColoredShape redCircle{circle, "red"};
redCircle.resize(2); // won't compile!
```

Suppose you don't really care whether you can compose objects at runtime or not, but you really *do* care about being able to access all the fields and member functions of a decorated object. Is it possible to construct such a decorator?

Well, in actual fact, it is, and it's done through templates and inheritance – but not the kind of inheritance that causes a state space explosion. Instead, we shall apply something called mixin inheritance, an approach when the class inherits from its own template argument.

So here's the idea – we'll make a new ColoredShape, one that inherits from a template parameter.

```
template <typename T> struct ColoredShape : T
{
  string color;

  string str() const override
  {
    ostringstream oss;
    oss << T::str() << " has the color " << color;
    return oss.str();
  }
}; // implementation of TransparentShape<T> omitted
```

One point of concern is how to make sure that the type parameter T inherits from shape. There are two options here:

- Use a static assert, that is,

  ```
  template <typename T> struct ColoredShape2 : T
  {
    static_assert(is_base_of_v<Shape, T>,
      "Template argument must be a Shape");
    // as before
  };
  ```

- Use concepts.

Armed with implementations of ColoredShape<T> and TransparentShape<T>, we can now compose them into a colored, transparent shape:

```
ColoredShape<TransparentShape<Square>> square{"blue"};
square.size = 2;
square.transparency = 0.5;
cout << square.str();
// can call square's own members
square.resize(3);
```

Isn't this great? Well, great but not perfect: we seem to have lost the full use of our constructors, so even though we are able to initialize the outermost class, we cannot fully construct a shape with specific size, color, and transparency in a single line of code.

To put the icing (decorations!) on our cake, let's give ColoredShape and TransparentShape forwarding constructors. These constructors will take two arguments: the first shall be the argument specific to the current template class, and the second will be a generic parameter pack that we'll forward to our base class. Here's what I mean:

```
template <typename T> struct TransparentShape : T
{
  uint8_t transparency;

  template<typename...Args>
  TransparentShape(const uint8_t transparency, Args...args)
    : T(std::forward<Args>(args)...)
    , transparency{ transparency } {}

  ...
}; // same for ColoredShape
```

Just to reiterate, this constructor can accept any number of arguments, where the first argument gets used to initialize the transparency value and the rest are simply forwarded to the constructor of the base class, whatever that happens to be. Unfortunately, the set of arguments has to be reversed.

The number of constructor parameters naturally has to be correct, and the program will fail to compile if their number or the types of values are incorrect. This also places certain restrictions on the way constructors can be called, since a forwarding constructor will always try to "fill" the available constructors depending on what's actually available. In situations where nested constructors have overloads, you may be unable to instantiate the objects you need with one-line syntax.

Oh, and be sure to never make these constructors explicit or you'll run afoul of C++'s copy-list-initialization rules when composing the decorators together. Now, how about actually using all this goodness?

```
ColoredShape<TransparentShape<Square>> sq{ "red", 51, 5 };
cout << sq.str();
// A square with side 5 has 20% transparency has the color red
```

Tada! As you can see, the constructor parameters get "distributed" among the constructors of the inheritance chain: the value "red" goes into ColoredShape, 51 goes into TransparentShape, and the value of 5 is fed to Square.

Functional Decorator

While the Decorator pattern is typically applied to classes, it can be equally applied to functions. For example, suppose there's a particular operation in your code that's giving you trouble: you want to record all the times when this is called and analyze the statistics in Excel. Well, this can certainly be done just by putting some code before and after the call, that is:

```
cout << "Entering function XYZ\n";
// do the work
cout << "Exiting function XYZ\n";
```

This works just fine, but isn't good in terms of Separation of Concerns: we really want to store the logging functionality somewhere so that we can reuse it and enhance it when necessary.

There are different approaches to how to do this. One approach is to simply feed the entire unit of work as a function to some logging component similar to the following:

```
struct Logger
{
  function<void()> func;
  string name;

  Logger(const function<void()>& func, const string& name)
    : func{func}, name{name} {}

  void operator()() const
  {
    cout << "Entering " << name << "\n";
    func();
    cout << "Exiting " << name << "\n";
  }
};
```

With this approach, you could write the following:

```
Logger([]() { cout << "Hello\n"; }, "HelloFunction")();
// Entering HelloFunction
// Hello
// Exiting HelloFunction
```

There is always an option of passing in the function not as an `std::function`, but as a template argument. This results in a slight variation of the preceding:

```
template <typename Func>
struct Logger2
{
  Func func;
  string name;

  Logger2(const Func& func, const string& name)
    : func{func}, name{name} {}

  void operator()() const
  {
    cout << "Entering " << name << endl;
    func();
    cout << "Exiting " << name << endl;
  }
};
```

The use of this implementation is exactly the same. We can make a utility function to actually create such a logger:

```
template <typename Func> auto make_logger2(Func func,
  const string& name)
{
  return Logger2<Func>{ func, name };
}
```

and then use it like this:

```
auto call = make_logger2([]() {cout << "Hello!" << endl; },
"HelloFunction");
call(); // output same as before
```

"What's the point?", you might ask. Well... we now have an ability to create a decorator (with the decorated function inside it) and to call it at the time of our choosing.

Now, here's a challenge for you: what if you wanted to log the invocation of the function add(), defined as follows:

```cpp
double add(double a, double b)
{
  cout << a << "+" << b << "=" << (a + b) << endl;
  return a + b;
}
```

but you also wanted to get the return value? Yep, a return value returned from the logger. Not so easy! But certainly not impossible. Let's make yet another incarnation of our logger:

```cpp
template <typename R, typename... Args>
struct Logger3<R(Args...)>
{
  Logger3(function<R(Args...)> func, const string& name)
    : func{func}, name{name} {}

  R operator() (Args ...args)
  {
    cout << "Entering " << name << endl;
    R result = func(args...);
    cout << "Exiting " << name << endl;
    return result;
  }

  function<R(Args ...)> func;
  string name;
};
```

In the preceding, the template argument R refers to the type of the return value, and Args refers to the types of arguments the function takes. The decorator holds on to the function and calls it when necessary; the only difference is that operator() returns an R, so you don't lose the return value.

We can construct another utility make_ function:

```
template <typename R, typename... Args>
auto make_logger3(R (*func)(Args...), const string& name)
{
  return Logger3<R(Args...)>(
    function<R(Args...)>(func),
    name);
}
```

And notice how, instead of going for an std::function, I've defined the first argument as an ordinary function pointer. We can now use this function to instantiate the logged invocation and use it:

```
auto logged_add = make_logger3(add, "Add");
auto result = logged_add(2, 3);
```

Of course, make_logger3 can be supplanted with dependency injection. The upside of this approach would be an ability to

- Dynamically turn logging on and off by providing a Null Object (see the corresponding chapter) instead of an actual logger.

- Disable the actual invocation of the code being logged (again, by substituting a different logger).

All in all, another useful tool on the developer's toolbelt. I leave the weaving of this approach into dependency injection as an exercise for the reader.

Summary

A decorator gives a class additional functionality while adhering to the OCP. Its crucial aspect is *composability*: several decorators can be applied to an object in any order. We've looked at the following types of decorators:

- *Dynamic decorators* which can store references (or even store the entire values, if you want!) of the decorated objects and provide dynamic (runtime) composability at the expense of not being able to access the underlying objects' own members.

- *Static decorators* use mixin inheritance (inheriting from template parameter) to compose decorators at compile time. This loses any sort of runtime flexibility (you cannot recompose objects) but gives you access to the underlying object's members. These objects are also fully initializable through constructor forwarding.

- *Functional decorators* can wrap either blocks of code or particular functions to allow composition of behaviors.

It's worth mentioning that in languages which do *not* allow multiple inheritance, decorators are also used to simulate it by aggregating more than one object and then providing an interface that is the set union of the interfaces of the aggregated objects.

CHAPTER 10

Façade

First, let's get the linguistic issue out of the way: that little hook on the letter Ç is called a *cedilla* and the letter itself is pronounced as an S, so the word "façade" is pronounced as *fah-saad*. The particularly pedantic among you are welcome to use the letter Ç/ç in your code, since most compilers treat it just fine, but you *will* need to save the source code in a suitable encoding (I recommend UTF-8) in order for the compiler to process it correctly.[1]

Now, about the pattern itself... essentially, the best analogy I can think of is a typical house. When you buy a house, you generally care about the exterior and the interior. You are less concerned about the internals: electrical systems, insulation, sanitation, that sort of thing. Those parts are all equally important, but we want them to "just work" without breaking. You're much more likely to be buying new furniture than changing the wiring of your boiler.

The same idea applies to software: sometimes you need to interact with a complicated system in a simple way. By "system" we could mean a set of components or just a single component with a rather complicated API.

---

[1] Over the years, I have seen many silly tricks involving the use of Unicode (typically UTF-8) encoding in source files. The most insidious case is one where a developer insisted on calling some identifiers this – it was, of course, a completely valid identifier because the letter i in this was a Ukrainian letter i, not a Latin one.

© Dmitri Nesteruk 2022
D. Nesteruk, *Design Patterns in Modern C++20*,
https://doi.org/10.1007/978-1-4842-7295-4_10

Magic Square Generator

While a proper Façade demo requires that we make super-complicated systems that actually warrant a Façade to be put in front of them, let us consider a trivialized example: the process of making magic squares. A magic square is a matrix such as

$$\begin{bmatrix} 1 & 14 & 14 & 4 \\ 11 & 8 & 6 & 9 \\ 8 & 10 & 10 & 5 \\ 13 & 2 & 3 & 15 \end{bmatrix}$$

If you add up the values in any row, any column, or any diagonal, you'll get the same number – in this case, 33. If we want to generate our own magic squares, we can imagine it as an interplay of three different subsystems:

- Generator: A component which simply generates a sequence of random numbers of a particular size

- Splitter: A component that takes a rectangular matrix and outputs a set of lists representing all rows, columns, and diagonals in the matrix

- Verifier: A component that checks that the sums of all lists passed into it are the same

We begin by implementing the Generator:

```
struct Generator
{
  virtual vector<int> generate(const int count) const
  {
    vector<int> result(count);
```

```
generate(result.begin(), result.end(),
  [&]() { return 1 + rand()%9; });
return result;
  }
}
```

The Generator can give us a vector of a particular size filled with random values generated by a particular algorithm. Here I use the simple rand() for brevity. To make a magic square, we call the generate() method N times to generate N rows, resulting in an N×N square.

The next component, called a Splitter, takes the generated 2D matrix and uses it to produce unique elements representing all the rows, columns, and diagonals of a matrix. For example, given an input matrix

$$\begin{bmatrix} 1 & 2 \\ 3 & 4 \end{bmatrix}$$

the splitter will produce the following set of values:

$$\begin{bmatrix} 1 & 2 \\ 3 & 4 \\ 1 & 3 \\ 2 & 4 \\ 1 & 4 \\ 2 & 3 \end{bmatrix}$$

These values represent all the rows, columns, and diagonals of the initial 2×2 matrix. The interface of the Splitter is the following:

```
struct Splitter
{
  vector<vector<int>> split(vector<vector<int>> array) const
  {
```

```
    // implementation omitted
  }
};
```

The implementation of Splitter is rather long-winded, so I've omitted it here – take a look at the source code for its exact details. As you can see, the Splitter returns a vector of vectors (a 2D matrix).

Our final component, Verifier, checks that those lists all add up to the same number:

```
struct Verifier
{
  bool verify(vector<vector<int>> array) const
  {
    if (array.empty()) return false;
    auto expected = accumulate(array[0].begin(),
      array[0].end(), 0);
    return all_of(array.begin(), array.end(), [=](auto& inner)
      {
        return accumulate(inner.begin(), inner.end(), 0) ==
        expected;
      });
  }
};
```

So there you have it – we have three different subsystems that are expected to work in concert in order to generate random magic squares. But are they easy to use? If we gave these classes to a client, they would really struggle to operate them correctly. So, how can we make their lives better?

The answer is simple: we build a Façade, essentially a wrapper class that hides all these implementation details and provides a very simple interface. Of course, it uses all the three classes behind the scenes:

```
struct MagicSquareGenerator
{
  vector<vector<int>> generate(int size)
  {
    Generator g;
    Splitter s;
    Verifier v;

    vector<vector<int>> square;

    do
    {
      square.clear();
      for (int i = 0; i < size; ++i)
        square.emplace_back(g.generate(size));
    } while (!v.verify(s.split(square)));

    return square;
  }
};
```

And there you have it! Now, if the client wants to generate a 3×3 magic square, all they have to do is call

```
MagicSquareGenerator gen;
auto square = gen.generate(3);
```

And they'll get something like

$$\begin{bmatrix} 3 & 1 & 5 \\ 5 & 3 & 1 \\ 1 & 5 & 3 \end{bmatrix}$$

Fine-Tuning

Quite often, you want to allow power users to customize and extend the behavior of a façade with additional features. For example, a magic square façade may wish to allow the user to provide a custom number generator. To implement this, first of all, we change Generate() to take each of the subsystems as template parameters:

```
template <typename G = Generator,
  typename S = Splitter,
  typename V = Verifier>
struct MagicSquareGenerator
{
  vector<vector<int>> generate(int size)
  {
    G g;
    S s;
    V v;
    // rest of code as before
  }
}
```

We could, if we wanted to, add further restrictions requiring that parameters G, S, and V inherit from the corresponding classes.

Now, if the user wants to ensure all the values in a row are unique, they can make a UniqueGenerator that ensures that all the numbers in the generated set are unique:

```
struct UniqueGenerator : Generator
{
  vector<int> generate(const int count) const override
  {
    vector<int> result;
```

```
do
{
    result = Generator::generate(count);
} while (set<int>(result.begin(),result.end()).size()
            != result.size());
return result;
    }
};
```

We can then feed this new generator into the Façade, thereby getting a different magic Square. Notice we only provide the first template parameter, using the defaults for Splitter and Verifier.

```
MagicSquareGenerator<UniqueGenerator> gen;
auto square = gen.generate(3);
```

This gives us

$$\begin{bmatrix} 8 & 1 & 6 \\ 3 & 5 & 7 \\ 4 & 9 & 2 \end{bmatrix}$$

Of course, it's really impractical to generate magic squares this way, but what this example demonstrates is that you can hide complicated interactions between different systems behind a Façade and that you can also incorporate a certain amount of configurability so that users can customize the internal operations of the mechanism should the need arise.

Building a Trading Terminal

I've spent a lot of time working in areas of quant finance and algorithmic trading. As you can probably guess, what's required of a good trading terminal is quick delivery of information into a trader's brain: you want things to be rendered as fast as possible, without any lag.

Most of financial data (except for the charts) is actually rendered in plain text: white characters on a black screen. This is, in a way, similar to the way the terminal/console/command-line interface works in your own operating system.

The first part of a terminal window is the *buffer*. This is where the rendered characters are stored. A buffer is a rectangular area of memory, typically a 1D[2] or 2D `char` or `wchar_t` array. A buffer can be much larger than the visible area of the terminal window, so it can store some historical output that you can scroll back to.

Typically, a buffer has a pointer (e.g., an integer) specifying the current input line. That way, a full buffer doesn't reallocate all lines; it just overwrites the oldest one.

Then there's the idea of a *viewport*. A viewport renders a part of the particular buffer. A buffer can be huge, so a viewport just takes a rectangular area out of that buffer and renders that. Naturally, the size of the viewport has to be less than or equal to the size of the buffer.

Finally, there's the console (terminal window) itself. The console shows the viewport, allows scrolling up and down, and even accepts user input. The console is, in fact, a façade: a simplified representation of what is a rather complicated set-up behind the scenes.

Typically, most users interact with a single buffer and viewport. It *is*, however, possible to have a console window where you have, say, the area split vertically between two viewports, each having their corresponding buffers. This can be done using utilities such as the `screen` Linux command.

---

[2] Most buffers are one dimensional. The reason for this is that it's easier to pass a single pointer somewhere than a double pointer, and using an `array` or `vector` doesn't make much sense when the size of the structure is deterministic and immutable. Another advantage to the 1D approach is that when it comes to GPU processing, platforms such as CUDA use up to six dimensions for addressing *anyway*, so after a while, computing a 1D index from an N-dimensional block/ grid position becomes second nature.

An Advanced Terminal

One problem with a typical operating system terminal is that it is *extremely slow* if you pipe a lot of data into it. For example, a Windows terminal window (cmd.exe) uses GDI to render the characters, which is completely unnecessary. In a fast-paced trading environment, you want the rendering to be hardware-accelerated: characters should be preseted as pre-rendered textures placed on a surface using an API such as OpenGL.[3]

A trading terminal consists of *multiple* buffers and viewports, as illustrated in Figure 10-1. In a typical set-up, different buffers might be getting updated concurrently with data from various exchanges or trading bots, and all of this information needs to be presented on a single screen.[4]

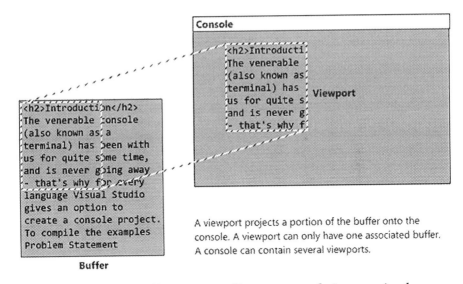

Figure 10-1. *Visual illustration of how a console is organized*

---

[3] We also use ASCII, since Unicode is rarely, if ever, required. Having 1 char = 1 byte is a good practice if you don't need to support extra character sets. While not relevant to the discussion at hand, it also greatly simplifies the implementation of string processing algorithms on both GPUs and CPUs.

[4] Actually, we use multiple screens, which makes the implementation even more challenging.

Buffers also provide functionality that is a lot more exciting than just a 1D or 2D linear storage. For example, a TableBuffer might be defined as

```
struct TableBuffer : Buffer
{
  TableBuffer(vector<TableColumnSpec> spec, int totalHeight) {
  ... }

  struct TableColumnSpec
  {
    string header;
    int width;
    enum class TableColumnAlignment {
      Left, Center, Right
    } alignment;
  }
};
```

In other words, a buffer can take some specification and build a table (yes, a food old-fashioned ASCII-formatted table!) and present it on screen.

A viewport is in charge of getting data from the buffer. Some of its characteristics include

- A reference to the buffer it's showing.

- Its size.

- If the viewport is smaller than the buffer, it needs to specify which part of the buffer it is going to show. This is expressed in absolute x-y coordinates.

- The location of the viewport on the overall console window.

- The location of the cursor, assuming this viewport is currently taking user input.

Where's the Façade?

The console itself *is* the façade in this particular system. Internally, the console has to manage many different objects:

```
struct Console
{
  vector<Viewport*> viewports;
  Size charSize, gridSize;

  ...
};
```

Initialization of the console is, typically, a very complicated affair. However, since it's a Façade, it actually tries to provide a really accessible API. This might either take a number of sensible parameters to initialize all the guts from.

```
Console::Console(bool fullscreen, int char_width, int char_
height,
  int width, int height, optional<Size> client_size)
{
  // single buffer and viewport created here
  // linked together and added to appropriate collections
  // image textures generated
  // grid size calculated depending on whether we want
     fullscreen mode
}
```

Alternatively, one might pack all the arguments into a single Parameter Object which, again, has some sensible defaults:

```
Console::Console(const ConsoleCreationParameters& ccp) { ... }
struct ConsoleCreationParameters
{
  optional<Size> client_size;
  int character_width{10};
  int character_height{14};
  int width{20};
  int height{30};
  bool fullscreen{false};
  bool create_default_view_and_buffer{true};
};
```

Naturally, any particular set of defaults can have dynamic and static variations:

- Dynamically provided parameters filled in a structure (as in our ConsoleCreationParameters) can be changed at runtime.

- Providers supplied statically as template arguments.

The choice of each depends on whether the values need to be mutable. For example, if the console doesn't support resizing, you can take width/height as template arguments, again, with sensible defaults.

Summary

The Façade design pattern is a way of putting a simple interface in front of one or more complicated subsystems. It provides for ease of use yet, at the same time, may expose customization points for power users to fine-tune the operation of the façade.

CHAPTER 11

Flyweight

A Flyweight (also sometimes called a *token* or a *cookie*) is a temporary component which acts as a "smart reference" to something. Typically, flyweights are used in situations where you have a very large number of very similar objects, and you want to minimize the amount of memory that is dedicated to storing all these values.

Let's take a look at some scenarios where this pattern becomes relevant.

User Names

Imagine a massively multiplayer online game. I bet you $20 there's more than one user called John Smith – quite simply because it is a popular name. So if we were to store that name over and over (in ASCII), we would be spending at least 11 bytes for every such user, possibly more. Instead, we could store the name once and then store a pointer to every user with that name. That's quite a saving assuming user names do repeat.

It would, perhaps, make even more sense to fragment the name into first and last names: that way, Fitzgerald Smith would be represented by two pointers, pointing to first and last names, respectively. In fact, we can cut down the number of bytes used if we use indices instead of pointers. You don't expect there to be 2^64 unique first and last names, do you?

© Dmitri Nesteruk 2022

D. Nesteruk, *Design Patterns in Modern C++20*,

https://doi.org/10.1007/978-1-4842-7295-4_11

To begin with, we can typedef a data type used for the key. We can also tweak it later.

```
typedef uint16_t key;
```

With this definition, we can make a user defined as follows:

```
struct User
{
  User(const string& first_name, const string& last_name)
    : first_name{add(first_name)}, last_name{add(last_name)} {}
  ⋮
protected:
  key first_name, last_name;
  static bimap<key, string> names;
  static key seed;
  static key add(const string& s) { ... }
};
```

As you can see, the constructor initializes the members first_name and last_name with the result of calling a private add() function. This function inserts the key-value pairs (keys are generated from a seed) into the names structure as necessary. I'm using a boost::bimap (bidirectional map) here, because it makes it easier to search for duplicates – remember, if the first or last name is already in the bimap, we just return an index to it.

So here is the implementation of the add() function:

```
static key User::add(const string& s)
{
  auto it = names.right.find(s);
  if (it == names.right.end())
  {
    // add it
    names.insert({++seed, s});
```

```
  return seed;
}
return it->second;
}
```

This is a fairly standard implementation of the get or add mechanic. You might want to consult bimap's documentation for more info on how it works if you haven't met it before.[1]

So now, if we want to actually *expose* the first and last names (the fields are protected and are of type key, not very useful!), we can provide the appropriate getters and setters:

```
const string& get_first_name() const
{
  return names.left.find(last_name)->second;
}

const string& get_last_name() const
{
  return names.left.find(last_name)->second;
}
```

For example, to define a User's stream output operator, you could simply write

```
friend ostream& operator<<(ostream& os, const User& obj)
{
  return os
    << "first_name: " << obj.get_first_name()
    << " last_name: " << obj.get_last_name();
}
```

---

[1]www.boost.org/doc/libs/1_73_0/libs/bimap/doc/html/index.html

And that's it. I am not going to offer statistics on the amount of space saved (this really depends on your sample size and how you choose to encode strings), but hopefully it's obvious that, in the case of a large number of repeating user names, the savings are significant – especially if you choose a smaller data type for the key.

Boost.Flyweight

In the previous example, I have hand-crafted a Flyweight even though I could have reused one available as a Boost library. The `boost::flyweight` type does exactly what it says on the tin: constructs a space-saving flyweight.

This makes the implementation of the User class rather trivial:

```
struct User2
{
  flyweight<string> first_name, last_name;

  User2(const string& first_name, const string& last_name)
    : first_name{first_name},
      last_name{last_name} {}
};
```

And you can verify that it *is* in fact a flyweight by running the following code:

```
User2 john_doe{ "John", "Doe" };
User2 jane_doe{ "Jane", "Doe" };
cout << boolalpha <<
  (&jane_doe.last_name.get() == &john_doe.last_name.get());
  // true
```

String Ranges

If we call `string::substring()`, should that return us a brand new constructed string? The jury is out: if you want to manipulate it then sure, but what if you want changes to the substring to affect the original object? Some programming languages (e.g., Swift, Rust) explicitly return a substring as a *range* which is, again, an implementation of the Flyweight pattern that saves on the amount of memory used, in addition to allowing us to manipulate the underlying object through the range.

The C++ equivalent to a range of a string is a `string_view`, and there are additional variations for arrays – anything to avoid copying data! In C++, `string_view` has made its appearance long after the `string` data type, and the way its use was incorporated was to allow an implicit conversion from a `string`, that is:

```
string s = "hello world!";
string_view sv = string_view(s).substr(0, 5);
```

We are going to construct our own, very trivial, string range. We shall assume that we've got some text stored in a containing class, and we want to grab a range of that text and capitalize it, kind of like something a word processor or IDE might do. We *could* just modify the underlying text and be done with it, but let's assume we want to keep the plain text in its original state and only capitalize letters for when we use the stream output operator.

Naïve Approach

A very silly way of solving the problem would be to define a `bool` array whose size matches the plain-text string, and the flags indicate whether we capitalize the character or not. We can implement it like this:

```
class FormattedText
{
  string plainText;
```

```
  bool *caps;
public:
  explicit FormattedText(const string& plainText)
    : plainText{plainText}
  {
    caps = new bool[plainText.length()];
  }
  ~FormattedText()
  {
    delete[] caps;
  }
};
```

We can now make a utility method for capitalizing a particular range of letters within a piece of text.

```
void capitalize(int start, int end)
{
  for (int i = start; i <= end; ++i)
    caps[i] = true;
}
```

Now we can define a stream output operator that makes use of the Boolean mask:

```
friend ostream& operator<<(ostream& os,
  const FormattedText& obj)
{
  string s;
  for (int i = 0; i < obj.plainText.length(); ++i)
  {
    char c = obj.plainText[i];
```

```
    s += (obj.caps[i] ? toupper(c) : c);
  }
  return os << s;
}
```

Don't get me wrong, this approach works:

```
FormattedText ft("This is a brave new world");
ft.capitalize(10, 15);
cout << ft; // This is a BRAVE new world
```

But, again, it's very silly to define every single character as having a Boolean flag, when just the start and end markers will do. This approach also fails to scale. Imagine if you also want to underline text or make it italic – in this case, you'd be introducing even more space-wasting Boolean arrays. Sure, Boolean values do support a certain amount of compactification (let's not mention vector<bool>!), but even so, this approach is wasteful.

Let us try to use the Flyweight pattern again.

Flyweight Implementation

Let's implement a BetterFormattedText that makes use of the Flyweight design pattern. We'll begin by defining both the outer class and the nested TextRange class that happens to be our Flyweight:

```
class BetterFormattedText
{
public:
  struct TextRange
  {
    int start, end;
    bool capitalize{false};
    // other options here, e.g. bold, italic, etc.
```

```
    // determine our range covers a particular position
    bool covers(int position) const
    {
      return position >= start && position <= end;
    }
  };
private:
  string plain_text;
  vector<TextRange> formatting;
};
```

As you can see, TextRange just stores the start and end points to which it applies, as well as the actual formatting information – whether we want to capitalize text as well as any other formatting option (e.g., bold, italic, etc.). It has just a single member function covers() that helps us determine whether this piece of formatting needs to be applied to the character at the given position.

BetterFormattedText stores a vector of TextRange flyweights and is able to construct new ones on demand:

```
TextRange& get_range(int start, int end)
{
  formatting.emplace_back(TextRange{ start, end });
  return *formatting.rbegin();
}
```

Three things are happening in this listing:

1. A new TextRange is constructed.

2. It gets moved into the vector.

3. A reference to the last element is returned.

We don't really check duplicate ranges in our implementation –
something that would also be in the spirit of Flyweight-based space economy.

We can now implement operator<< for BetterFormattedText:

```
friend ostream& operator<<(ostream& os,
  const BetterFormattedText& obj)
{
  string s;
  for (size_t i = 0; i < obj.plain_text.length(); i++)
  {
    auto c = obj.plain_text[i];
    for (const auto& rng : obj.formatting)
    {
      if (rng.covers(i) && rng.capitalize)
        c = toupper(c);
      s += c;
    }
  }
  return os << s;
}
```

Again, all we do is go through each character and check whether
there's any range that covers it. If there is, we apply whatever the range
specifies, in our case, capitalization. Note that this set-up allows ranges
to freely overlap. Naturally, such a linear search over every single range
is inefficient, but we'll let it happen here because we're concerned with
memory savings rather than performance.

We can now use all that we've constructed to capitalize that same word
as before, albeit with a slightly different, more flexible, API:

```
BetterFormattedText bft("This is a brave new world");
bft.get_range(10, 15).capitalize = true;
cout << bft; // This is a BRAVE new world
```

Summary

The Flyweight pattern is fundamentally a space-saving technique. Its exact incarnations are diverse: sometimes you have the Flyweight being returned as an API token that allows you to perform modifications of whoever has spawned it, and sometimes the Flyweight is implicit, hiding behind the scenes – as in the case of our User, where the client isn't meant to know about the Flyweight actually being used.

CHAPTER 12

Proxy

When we looked at the Decorator design pattern, we saw the different ways of enhancing the functionality of an object. The Proxy design pattern is similar, but its goal is to preserve exactly (or as closely as possible) the API that is being used while offering certain internal enhancements.

Proxy isn't a homogeneous pattern because the different kinds of proxies people build are quite numerous and serve entirely different purposes. In this chapter, we'll take a look at a selection of different proxy objects, and you can find more online and in literature.

Smart Pointers

The simplest and most direct illustration of the Proxy pattern is a smart pointer. A smart pointer is a wrapper for a pointer that also keeps a reference count and overrides certain operators, but all in all, it provides you the interface that you would get in an ordinary pointer:

```cpp
struct BankAccount
{
  void deposit(int amount) { ... }
};

BankAccount *ba = new BankAccount;
ba->deposit(123);
auto ba2 = make_shared<BankAccount>();
ba2->deposit(123); // same API!
```

© Dmitri Nesteruk 2022
D. Nesteruk, *Design Patterns in Modern C++20*,
https://doi.org/10.1007/978-1-4842-7295-4_12

So a smart pointer can also be used as a substitute in locations where an ordinary pointer is expected. For example, if (ba) { ... } is valid whether ba is a pointer or a smart pointer. *ba will, in both cases, get you the underlying object. And so on.

There are, of course, differences, the most obvious one being that you don't have to call delete on a smart pointer. But apart from that, it really tries to be as close to an ordinary pointer as possible.

Property Proxy

The term *property* in other programming languages is used to indicate a combination of a (backing) field together with getter/setter methods for that field. There is no built-in property support in C++;[1] the most common approach is to create a pair of get/set methods with names similar to the underlying field. However, this implies that to manipulate x.foo, we would have to call x.get_foo() and x.set_foo(value), respectively. But if we want to keep using field access syntax (i.e., keep writing x.foo) while giving it particular accessor/mutator behaviors, we can build a *property proxy*.

Essentially, a property proxy is a class that can masquerade as an ordinary field in terms of usage semantics. We can define it like this:

```
template <typename T> struct Property
{
  T value;
  Property(const T initial_value)
  {
    *this = initial_value; // invokes operator =
  }
}
```

---

[1] If you are happy with non-standard C++, check out the __declspec(property) extension, which is implemented in many modern compilers including Clang, MSVC, and GCC.

```
  operator T()
  {
    // perform some getter action
    return value;
  }
  T operator =(T new_value)
  {
    // perform some setter action
    return value = new_value;
  }
};
```

In the preceding implementation, I've added comments in places that you would typically customize (or replace outright), which correspond roughly to the location of getters/setters. One possible customization, for example, would be to put additional notification code in the setter so as to implement observable properties (as per the Observer pattern).

Our class Property<T> is, essentially, a drop-in replacement for the underlying T, whatever that happens to be. It works by simply allowing conversion to and from T, letting both use the value field behind the scenes. You can now replace an ordinary field with this type:

```
struct Creature
{
  Property<int> strength{ 10 };
  Property<int> agility{ 5 };
};
```

And the typical operations on a field will work also on a field of a property proxy type:

```
Creature creature;
creature.agility = 20;     // calls Property<int>::operator =
auto x = creature.strength; // calls Property<int>::operator T
```

One possible extension to the property proxy is to introduce pseudo strong typing, perhaps by having a `Property<T, int Tag>` so that values with different intentions are defined by different types. This is useful if, for example, you want to support some sort of arithmetic on like types so that, for example, two `strength` values can be added together, but `strength` and `agility` values cannot.

Virtual Proxy

If you try to dereference a `nullptr` or an uninitialized pointer, you're asking for trouble. However, there are situations where you only want the object constructed when it's accessed, and you don't want to allocate it prematurely, thus keeping it as a `nullptr` or similar until the time comes to actually use it.

This approach is called *lazy instantiation* or *lazy loading*. If you know exactly where you're going to need lazy behaviors, you can plan ahead and make special provisions for them. But if you don't, you can build a proxy that takes an existing object and makes it lazy. We call this a *virtual* proxy because the underlying object might not even exist, so instead of accessing something concrete, we're accessing something virtual.

Imagine a typical Image interface:

```
struct Image
{
  virtual void draw() = 0;
};
```

An eager (opposite of lazy) implementation of a `Bitmap`, which implements the `Image` interface, would load the image from a file on construction, even if that image isn't actually required for anything. (And yes, the following code is an emulation.)

```
struct Bitmap : Image
{
  Bitmap(const string& filename)
  {
    cout << "Loading image from " << filename << endl;
    // image gets loaded here
  }

  void draw() override
  {
    cout << "Drawing image " << filename << endl;
  }
};
```

The very act of constructing this Bitmap will trigger the loading of the image:

```
Bitmap img{ "pokemon.png" }; // Loading image from pokemon.png
```

That's not quite what we want. What we want is a kind of bitmap that only loads itself when the draw() method is called. Now, I suppose we could jump back into Bitmap and make it lazy, but let us assume it is set in stone and is not modifiable (or inheritable, for that matter).

What we can do in this situation is build a virtual proxy that will aggregate the original Bitmap, provide an identical interface, and also reuse the original Bitmap's functionality:

```
struct LazyBitmap : Image
{
  LazyBitmap(const string& filename)
    : filename(filename) {}
  ~LazyBitmap() { delete bmp; }
  void draw() override
  {
```

```
    if (!bmp)
      bmp = new Bitmap(filename);
    bmp->draw();
  }
private:
  Bitmap *bmp{nullptr};
  string filename;
};
```

Here we are. As you can see, the constructor of this LazyBitmap is a lot less "heavy": all it does is store the name of the file to load the image from, and that's it – the image doesn't get loaded immediately.

All of the magic happens in draw(): this is where we check the bmp pointer to see whether the underlying (eager!) bitmap has been constructed. If it hasn't, we construct it and then call its draw() function to actually draw the image.

Now suppose we have some API that uses an Image type:

```
void draw_image(Image& img)
{
  cout << "About to draw the image" << endl;
  img.draw();
  cout << "Done drawing the image" << endl;
}
```

We can use that API with an instance of LazyBitmap instead of Bitmap (hooray, polymorphism!) to render the image, loading it in a lazy fashion:

```
LazyBitmap img{ "pokemon.png" };
draw_image(img); // image loaded here

// About to draw the image
// Loading image from pokemon.png
```

```
// Drawing image pokemon.png
// Done drawing the image
```

That's it, our virtual proxy allows us to do lazy loading!

Communication Proxy

Suppose you call a member function foo() on an object of type Bar. Your typical assumption is that Bar has been allocated on the same machine as the one running your code, and you similarly expect Bar::foo() to execute in the same process.

Now, imagine that you make a design decision to move Bar and all its members off to a different machine on the network. But you still want the old code to work! If you want to keep going as before, you'll need a *communication proxy* – a component that proxies the calls "over the wire" and of course collects results, if necessary.

Let's implement a simple ping pong service to illustrate this. First, we define an interface:

```
struct Pingable
{
  virtual wstring ping(const wstring& message) = 0;
};
```

If we are building ping pong in-process, we can implement Pong as follows:

```
struct Pong : Pingable
{
  wstring ping(const wstring& message) override
  {
    return message + L" pong";
  }
};
```

Basically, you ping a Pong and it appends the word " pong" to the end of the message and returns that message. Notice how I'm not using an ostringstream& here, but instead making a new string on each turn: this API is simple to replicate as a web service.

We can now try out this set-up and see how it works in-process:

```
void tryit(Pingable& pp)
{
  wcout << pp.ping(L"ping") << "\n";
}

Pong pp;
for (int i = 0; i < 3; ++i)
{
  tryit(pp);
}
```

The end result is that we print "ping pong" three times, just as we wanted.

So now, suppose you decide to relocate the Pingable service to a web server far, far away. Perhaps you even decide to use some other platform, such as ASP.NET, instead of C++:

```
[Route("api/[controller]")]
public class PingPongController : Controller
{
  [HttpGet("{msg}")]
  public string Get(string msg)
  {
    return msg + " pong";
  }
} // achievement unlocked: use C# in a C++ book
```

With this set-up, we'll build a communication proxy called RemotePong that will be used in place of Pong. Microsoft's REST SDK comes in handy here.[2]

```cpp
struct RemotePong : Pingable
{
  wstring ping(const wstring& message) override
  {
    wstring result;
    http_client client(U("http://localhost:9149/"));
    uri_builder builder(U("/api/pingpong/"));
    builder.append(message);
    pplx::task<wstring> task = client.request(
      methods::GET, builder.to_string())
      .then([=](http_response r)
      {
        return r.extract_string();
      });
    task.wait();
    return task.get();
  }
};
```

If you are not used to the REST SDK, the preceding code might seem a little bewildering; in addition to REST support, the SDK uses the Concurrency Runtime, a Microsoft library for, you guessed it, concurrency support.

---

[2] The Microsoft REST SDK is a C++ library for working with REST services. It is both open source and cross-platform. You can find it on GitHub: https://github.com/Microsoft/cpprestsdk

With this implemented, we can now make a single change:

```
RemotePong pp; // was Pong
for (int i = 0; i < 3; ++i)
{
  tryit(pp);
}
```

And that's it, you get the same output, but the actual implementation can be running on ASP.NET in a Docker container somewhere halfway around the world.

Value Proxy

A value proxy is, as the name suggests, a proxy for a single value. Value proxies typically wrap primitive types and provide augmented functionality depending on their use.

Consider an example where you need to pass some values into a function. The function may take concrete, fixed values, but it can also take a *random* value from a predefined set, with a concrete value chosen at runtime.

One approach would be to modify this function and introduce several overloads, but, instead, we are going to modify the function parameter types. Let us introduce a helper class Value<T>:

```
template <typename T> struct Value
{
    virtual operator T() const = 0;
};
```

This class has only one pure virtual member that performs an implicit cast to type T whenever the compiler feels like such a cast could be useful.

On the basis of this, we can introduce a class Const<T> that represents a constant value:

```
template <typename T> struct Const : Value<T>
{
  const T v;

  Const() : v{} {}
  Const(T v) : v{v} {}

  operator T() const override
  {
    return v;
  }
};
```

This class acts as a wrapper for type T and will return the contained value whenever someone asks for it. Also notice that its constructors are not explicit. This means we can use it like this:

```
const Const<int> life{42};
cout << life/2 << "\n"; // 21
```

In a similar fashion, we can inherit Value<T> to introduce a value that is chosen randomly among several different options, each having equal probability:

```
template <typename T> struct OneOf : Value<T>
{
  vector<T> values;

  OneOf() : values{{T{}}} {} // :)
  OneOf(initializer_list<T> values) : values{values} {}

  operator T() const override
  {
```

```
    return values[rand() % values.size()];
  }
};
```

This allows us to initialize the container with a bunch of values and have it produce one at random whenever someone asks for it:

```
OneOf<int> stuff{ 1, 3, 5 };
cout << stuff << "\n"; // will print 1, 3 or 5
```

We can now make use of these types in an application. For example, say, you're testing a new dark theme for your application. You don't know whether your clients will like it, though. You can define a function such as

```
void draw_ui(const Value<bool>& use_dark_theme)
{
  if (use_dark_theme)
    cout << "Using dark theme\n";
  else
    cout << "Using normal theme\n";
}
```

Now, while you perform A/B testing, you can call the function as follows:

```
OneOf<bool> dark{true, false};
draw_ui(dark);
```

Once you know your users do like the dark theme better, you can simply replace the variable with a Const and you're done:

```
Const<bool> dark{true};
draw_ui(dark);
```

Notice that, unfortunately, there is no way to simply call draw_ui(true) because there are no implicit conversions from bool to const Value<bool>&.

The alternative is that you specify the receiving function "normally":

```
void draw_ui(bool use_dark_theme)
{
  if (use_dark_theme)
    cout << "Using dark theme\n";
  else
    cout << "Using normal theme\n";
}
```

And then proceed to specify the argument at the call site, that is:

```
OneOf<bool> dark{true, false};
draw_ui(dark);
// or
draw_ui(true);
```

The difference between the two approaches is obvious.

In the case where you pass a reference to a Value, you need to keep operating on objects within the hierarchy, but inside the function, you can use the implicit conversion to generate values more than once – and these values can be different on each call!

On the other hand, the use of Value at the call site means you can replace it with a literal such as true without loss of generality. This approach also follows the principle of least surprise since any client that sees a Value<T> as a parameter type will have to waste precious time searching for this hierarchy of types and learning how to work with it.

Summary

This chapter has presented a number of proxies. Unlike the Decorator pattern, the Proxy doesn't try to expand the functionality of an object by adding new members (unless it can't be helped) – all it tries to do is enhance the underlying behavior of existing members. A proxy is intended as a drop-in replacement.

Plenty of different proxies exist:

- Property proxies are stand-in objects that can replace fields and perform additional operations during assignment and/or access.

- Value proxies replace individual (scalar) values while augmenting them with additional functionality.

- Virtual proxies provide virtual access to the underlying object and can implement behaviors such as lazy loading. You may feel like you're working with a real object, but the underlying implementation may not have been created yet and can, for example, be loaded on demand.

- Communication proxies allow us to change the physical location of the object (e.g., move it to the cloud) but allow us to use the same API.

- Logging proxies allow you to perform logging in addition to calling the underlying functions.

There are lots of other proxies out there, and chances are that the ones you build yourself will not fall into a pre-existing category, but will, instead, perform some action specific to your domain.

PART III

Behavioral Patterns

When most people hear about behavioral patterns, it's primarily mentioned in the field of psychology, and the idea of getting people or animals to do what you want. Well, in a way, all of coding is about programs doing what you want, so behavioral software design patterns cover a very wide range of behaviors that are, nonetheless, quite common in programming.

As an example, consider the domain of software engineering. We have languages that are compiled, which involves lexing, parsing, and a million other things (the Interpreter pattern) and, having constructed an abstract syntax tree (AST) for a program, we might want to analyze the program for possible bugs (the Visitor pattern). All of these are behaviors that are common enough to be expressed as patterns, and this is why we are here today.

Unlike Creational patterns (which are concerned exclusively with the creation of objects) or Structural patterns (which are concerned with composition/aggregation/inheritance of objects), Behavioral design patterns do not follow a central theme. While there are certain similarities between different patterns (e.g., Strategy and Template Method do the same thing in different ways), most patterns present unique approaches to solving particular problems.

CHAPTER 13

Chain of Responsibility

Consider the typical example of corporate malpractice: insider trading, when a trader has been caught red-handed trading on inside information. Who is to blame for this? If management didn't know, it's the trader. But maybe the trader's peers were in on it, in which case the group manager might be the one responsible. Or perhaps the practice is institutional, in which case it's the CEO who would take the blame.

This is an example of a responsibility chain: you have several different elements of a system that can all process a message, one after another. As a concept, it's rather easy to implement, since all that's implied is the use of a list.

Scenario

Imagine a computer game where each creature has a name and two characteristic values – attack and defense:

```
struct Creature
{
  string name;
  int attack, defense;
  // constructor and << here
};
```

© Dmitri Nesteruk 2022
D. Nesteruk, *Design Patterns in Modern C++20*,
https://doi.org/10.1007/978-1-4842-7295-4_13

As the creature progresses through the game, it might acquire an item (e.g., a magic sword), or it might end up getting enchanted. In either case, its attack and defense values will be modified by something we'll call a CreatureModifier.

Furthermore, situations where *several* modifiers are applied are not uncommon, so we need to be able to stack modifiers on top of one another, allowing them to be applied in the order they were attached.

Let's see how we can implement this.

Pointer Chain

We shall implement CreatureModifier as follows:

```
class CreatureModifier
{
  CreatureModifier* next{nullptr};
protected:
  Creature& creature; // alternative: pointer or shared_ptr
public:
  explicit CreatureModifier(Creature& creature)
    : creature(creature) {}

  void add(CreatureModifier* cm)
  {
    if (next) next->add(cm);
    else next = cm;
  }

  virtual void handle()
  {
    if (next) next->handle(); // critical!
  }
};
```

There are a lot of things happening here, so let's discuss them in turn:

- The class takes and stores a reference to the Creature it plans to modify.

- The class doesn't really do much, but it's not abstract: all its members have implementations.

- The next member points to an optional CreatureModifier following this one. The implication is, of course, that the modifier it points to is an inheritor of CreatureModifier.

- The function add() adds another creature modifier to the modifier chain. This is done recursively: if the current modifier is nullptr, we set it to that; otherwise, we traverse the entire chain and put it on the end.

- The function handle() simply handles the next item in the chain, if it exists; it has no behavior of its own. The fact that it's virtual implies that it's meant to be overridden.

So far, all we have is an implementation of a poor man's append-only singly linked list. But when we start inheriting from it, things will hopefully become more clear. For example, here is how you would make a modifier that would double the creature's attack value:

```
class DoubleAttackModifier : public CreatureModifier
{
public:
  explicit DoubleAttackModifier(Creature& creature)
    : CreatureModifier(creature) {}

  void handle() override
  {
```

```
    creature.attack *= 2;
    CreatureModifier::handle();
  }
};
```

Alright, finally we're getting somewhere. This modifier inherits from CreatureModifier and in its handle() method does two things: doubles the attack value and calls handle() from the base class. The second part is critical: the only way in which a *chain* of modifiers can be applied is if every inheritor doesn't forget to call the base at the end of its own handle() implementation.

Here is another, more complicated modifier. This modifier increases the defense of creatures with attack of 2 or less by 1:

```
class IncreaseDefenseModifier : public CreatureModifier
{
public:
  explicit IncreaseDefenseModifier(Creature& creature)
    : CreatureModifier(creature) {}

  void handle() override
  {
    if (creature.attack <= 2) creature.defense += 1;
    CreatureModifier::handle();
  }
};
```

Again we call the base class at the end. Putting it all together, we can now make a creature and apply a combination of modifiers to it:

```
Creature goblin{ "Goblin", 1, 1 };
CreatureModifier root{ goblin };
DoubleAttackModifier r1{ goblin };
```

```
DoubleAttackModifier r1_2{ goblin };
IncreaseDefenseModifier r2{ goblin };

root.add(&r1);
root.add(&r1_2);
root.add(&r2);

root.handle();

cout << goblin << endl;
// name: Goblin attack: 4 defense: 1
```

As you can see, the goblin is a 4/1 because its attack got doubled twice and the defense modifier, while added, did not affect its defense score.

Here's another curious point. Suppose you decide to cast a spell on a creature such that no bonus can be applied to it. Is it easy to do? Quite easy, actually, because all you have to do is avoid calling the base handle(). This avoids executing the entire chain:

```
class NoBonusesModifier : public CreatureModifier
{
public:
  explicit NoBonusesModifier(Creature& creature)
    : CreatureModifier(creature) {}

  void handle() override
  {
    // nothing here!
  }
};
```

That's it! Now, if you slot the NoBonusesModifier at the *beginning* of the chain, no further elements will be applied. This raises an interesting point regarding how a Chain of Responsibility (CoR) will be treated. In most cases, you'll encounter Chain of Responsibility as a singly linked list with items appended onto the end. But in some cases, you can customize this list, for example, sorting items by priority in some sort of map<int, Modifier*> or similar structure.

Broker Chain

The example with the pointer chain is very artificial. In the real world, you'd want creatures to be able to take on and lose bonuses arbitrarily, something which an append-only linked list does not support. Furthermore, you don't want to modify the underlying creature stats permanently (as we did) – instead, you want to keep modifications temporary.

One way to implement Chain of Responsibility is through a centralized component. This component can keep a list of *all* modifiers available in the game and can facilitate queries for a particular creature's attack or defense by ensuring that all relevant bonuses are applied.

The component that we are going to build is called an *event broker*. Since it's connected to every participating component, it represents the Mediator design pattern, and, further, since it responds to queries through events, it leverages the Observer design pattern that is discussed later in the book.

Let's build one. First of all, we'll define a structure called Game that will represent, well, a game that's being played:

```
struct Game // mediator
{
  signal<void(Query&)> queries;
};
```

We are using Boost.Signals2 library for keeping a *signal* called queries. What this lets us do is fire this signal and have it handled by ever slot (listening component). But what do events have to do with querying a creature's attack or defense?

Well, imagine that you want to query a creature's statistic. You could certainly try to read a field, but remember – we need to apply all the modifiers before the final value is known. So instead we'll encapsulate a query in a separate object (this is the Command pattern[1]) defined as follows:

```
struct Query
{
  string creature_name;
  enum Argument { attack, defense } argument;
  int result;
};
```

What we've done here is encapsulated the concept of querying a particular value from a creature. To make a query, we need to provide the name of the creature and specify which statistic we're interested in. It is precisely this value (well, a reference to it) that will be constructed and used by Game::queries to apply the modifiers and return the final value.

Now, let's move on to the definition of Creature. It is very similar to what we had before. The only difference in terms of fields is a reference to a Game:

```
class Creature
{
  Game& game;
  int attack, defense;
public:
  string name;
```

---

[1] Actually, there's a bit of confusion here. The concept of Command Query Separation (CQS) suggests the separation of operations into commands (which mutate state and yield no value) and queries (which do not mutate anything but yield a value). The GoF does not have a concept of a Query, so we let *any* encapsulated instruction to a component be called a Command.

```
Creature(Game& game, ...) : game{game}, ... { ... }
// other members here
};
```

Now, notice how attack and defense are private. This means that to get at the *final* (post-modifier) attack value, you would need to call a separate getter function, for example:

```
int Creature::get_attack() const
{
  Query q{ name, Query::Argument::attack, attack };
  game.queries(q);
  return q.result;
}
```

This is where the magic happens! Instead of just returning a value or statically applying some pointer-based chain, what we do is create a Query with the right arguments and then send the query off to be handled by whoever is subscribed to Game::queries. Every single subscribed component gets a chance to modify the baseline attack value.

So let's now implement the modifiers. Once again, we'll make a base class, but this time around, it won't have a handle() method:

```
class CreatureModifier
{
  Game& game;
  Creature& creature;
public:
  CreatureModifier(Game& game, Creature& creature)
    : game(game), creature(creature) {}
};
```

The modifier base class isn't particularly interesting. In fact, you could get away with not using it at all, since all it does is ensure that the constructor is called with the right arguments. But since we've gone with this approach, let's now inherit CreatureModifier and see how one would perform actual modifications:

```
class DoubleAttackModifier : public CreatureModifier
{
  connection conn;
public:
  DoubleAttackModifier(Game& game, Creature& creature)
    : CreatureModifier(game, creature)
  {
    conn = game.queries.connect([&](Query& q)
    {
      if (q.creature_name == creature.name &&
        q.argument == Query::Argument::attack)
        q.result *= 2;
    });
  }

  ~DoubleAttackModifier() { conn.disconnect(); }
};
```

All the magic happens in the constructor (and destructor); no additional methods are required. In the constructor, we use the Game reference to grab hold of the Game::queries signal and connect to it, specifying a lambda that doubles the attack. Naturally, the lambda must make a couple of checks: we need to make sure that we are augmenting the right creature (we compare by name) and that the statistic we're after is, in fact, attack. Both pieces of information are kept inside the Query reference, as is the initial result value that we modify.

We also take care to store the signal connection so that we break it when the object is destroyed. This way, we can apply the modifier temporarily and let it fizzle out when, for example, the modifier goes out of scope.

Putting it all together, we get the following:

```
Game game;
Creature goblin{ game, "Strong Goblin", 2, 2 };
cout << goblin;
// name: Strong Goblin attack: 2 defense: 2
{
  DoubleAttackModifier dam{ game, goblin };
  cout << goblin;
  // name: Strong Goblin attack: 4 defense: 2
}
cout << goblin;
// name: Strong Goblin attack: 2 defense: 2
```

What's happening here? Well, prior to being modified, the goblin is a 2/2. Then, we manufacture a scope, within which the goblin is affected by a DoubleAttackModifier, so inside the scope, it is a 4/2 creature. As soon as we exit the scope, the modifier's destructor triggers and it disconnects itself from the broker, thus no longer affecting the values when they are queried. Consequently, the goblin reverts to being a 2/2 creature once again.

Summary

Chain of Responsibility is a very simple design pattern that lets components process a command (or a query) in turn. The simplest implementation of CoR is one where you simply make a pointer chain, and, in theory, you could replace it with just an ordinary vector or, perhaps, a list if you wanted fast removal as well.

A more sophisticated Broker Chain implementation that also leverages Mediator and Observer patterns allows us to process queries on an event (signal), letting each subscriber perform modifications of the originally passed object (it's a single reference that goes through the entire chain) before the final values are returned to the client.

CHAPTER 14

Command

Think about a trivial variable assignment, such as `meaningOfLife = 42`. The variable got assigned, but there's no record anywhere that the assignment took place. Nobody can give us the previous value. We cannot take the *fact* of assignment and serialize it somewhere. This is problematic, because without a record of the change, we are unable to roll back to previous values, perform audits, or do history-based debugging.[1]

The Command design pattern proposes that instead of working with objects directly by manipulating them through their APIs, we send them *commands*: instructions on how to do something. A command is nothing more than a data class with its members describing what to do and how to do it. Let's take a look at a typical scenario.

Scenario

Let's try to model a typical bank account that has a balance and an overdraft limit. We'll implement `deposit()` and `withdraw()` functions on it:

```
struct BankAccount
{
  int balance = 0;
  int overdraft_limit = -500;
```

---

[1] We *do* have dedicated historical debugging tools such as Visual Studio's IntelliTrace.

© Dmitri Nesteruk 2022
D. Nesteruk, *Design Patterns in Modern C++20*,
https://doi.org/10.1007/978-1-4842-7295-4_14

```
  void deposit(int amount)
  {
    balance += amount;
    cout << "deposited " << amount << ", balance is now " <<
      balance << "\n";
  }

  void withdraw(int amount)
  {
    if (balance - amount >= overdraft_limit)
    {
      balance -= amount;
      cout << "withdrew " << amount << ", balance is now " <<
        balance << "\n";
    }
  }
};
```

Now we can call the member functions directly, of course, but let us suppose that, for audit purposes, we need to make a record of every deposit and withdrawal made, and we cannot do it right inside BankAccount because – guess what – we've already designed, implemented, and tested that class.

Implementing the Command Pattern

We'll begin by defining an interface for a command.

```
struct Command
{
  virtual void call() const = 0;
};
```

Having made the interface, we can now use it to define a
BankAccountCommand that will encapsulate information about what to do
with a bank account:

```
struct BankAccountCommand : Command
{
  BankAccount& account;
  enum Action { deposit, withdraw } action;
  int amount;

  BankAccountCommand(BankAccount& account, const Action action,
    const int amount)
    : account(account), action(action), amount(amount) {}
```

The information contained in the command includes the following:

- The account to operate upon.

- The action to take; both the set of options and the
  variable to store those options are defined in a single
  declaration.

- The amount to deposit or withdraw.

Once the client provides this information, we can take it and use it to
perform the deposit or withdrawal:

```
void call() const override
{
  switch (action)
  {
  case deposit:
    account.deposit(amount);
    break;
```

```
case withdraw:
  account.withdraw(amount);
  break;
  }
}
```

With this approach, we can create the command and then perform modifications of the account right on the command:

```
BankAccount ba;
Command cmd{ba, BankAccountCommand::deposit, 100};
cmd.call();
```

This will deposit 100 dollars into our account. Easy! And if you're worried that we're still exposing the original deposit() and withdraw() member functions to the client, you can make them private and simply designate BankAccountCommand as a friend class.

Undo Operations

Since a command encapsulates all information about some modification of a BankAccount, it can equally roll back this modification and return its target object to its previous state.

To begin with, we need to decide whether to stick undo-related operations into our Command interface. I will do it here for purposes of brevity, but in general, this is a design decision that needs to respect the Interface Segregation Principle that we discussed at the beginning of the book. For example, if you envisage some commands being final and not subject to undo mechanics, it might make sense to split Command into, say, Callable and Undoable.

Anyways, here's the updated Command; note I have deliberately removed const from the functions:

```
struct Command
{
  virtual void call() = 0;
  virtual void undo() = 0;
};
```

And here is a naïve implementation of BankAccountCommand::undo(), motivated by the (incorrect, but working) assumption that account deposit and withdrawal are symmetric operations:

```
void undo() override
{
  switch (action)
  {
  case withdraw:
    account.deposit(amount);
    break;
  case deposit:
    account.withdraw(amount);
    break;
  }
}
```

Why is this implementation broken? Because if you tried to withdraw an amount equal to the GDP of a developed nation, you would not be successful, but when rolling back the transaction, we don't have a way of telling that it failed!

To get this information, we modify `withdraw()` to return a success flag:

```
bool withdraw(int amount)
{
  if (balance - amount >= overdraft_limit)
  {
    balance -= amount;
    cout << "withdrew " << amount << ", balance now " <<
      balance << "\n";
    return true;
  }
  return false;
}
```

That's much better! We can now modify the entire `BankAccountCommand` to do two things:

- Set a `success` flag when a withdrawal is made.

- Use this flag when `undo()` is called.

Here we go:

```
struct BankAccountCommand : Command
{
  ...
  bool withdrawal_succeeded;

  BankAccountCommand(BankAccount& account, const Action action,
    const int amount)
    : ..., withdrawal_succeeded{false} {}

  void call() override
  {
    switch (action)
    {
```

```
    ...
  case withdraw:
    withdrawal_succeeded = account.withdraw(amount);
    break;
  }
}
```

Do you now see why I removed const from the members of Command? Now that we are assigning a member variable withdrawal_succeeded, we can no longer claim that call() is const. I suppose I could have kept it on undo(), but there's very little benefit in that.

Okay, so now we have the flag, we can improve our implementation of undo():

```
void undo() override
{
  switch (action)
  {
  case withdraw:
    if (withdrawal_succeeded)
      account.deposit(amount);
    break;
    ...
  }
}
```

Tada! We can finally undo withdraw commands in a consistent fashion.

The goal of this exercise was, of course, to illustrate that in addition to storing information about the action to perform, a Command can also store some intermediate information that is useful for things like audits: if you detect a series of 100 failed withdrawal attempts, you can investigate a potential hack.

Composite Command

A transfer of money from account A to account B can be simulated with two commands:

1. Withdraw $X from A

2. Deposit $X to B

It would be nice if instead of creating and calling these two commands, we could just create and call a single command that encapsulates both of them. This is the essence of the Composite design pattern that we'll discuss later.

Let's define a skeleton composite command. I'm going to inherit from vector <BankAccountCommand> – this can be problematic since std::vector doesn't have a virtual destructor, but it's not a problem in our case. So here is a very simple definition:

```
struct CompositeBankAccountCommand :
vector<BankAccountCommand>, Command
{
  CompositeBankAccountCommand(const initializer_list<value_
  type>& items)
    : vector<BankAccountCommand>(items) {}

  void call() override
  {
    for (auto& cmd : *this)
      cmd.call();
  }
}
```

```
  void undo() override
  {
    for (auto it = rbegin(); it != rend(); ++it)
      it->undo();
  }
};
```

The `CompositeBankAccountCommand` is both a vector and a `Command`, which fits the definition of the Composite design pattern. I've added a constructor that takes an initializer list (very useful!) and implemented both `undo()` and `redo()` operations. Note that the `undo()` process goes through commands in reverse order; hopefully I don't have to explain *why* you'd want this as default behavior.

So now, how about a composite command specifically for transferring money? I would define it as follows:

```
struct MoneyTransferCommand : CompositeBankAccountCommand
{
  MoneyTransferCommand(BankAccount& from,
    BankAccount& to, int amount) :
  CompositeBankAccountCommand
    {
      BankAccountCommand{from, BankAccountCommand::withdraw,
      amount},
      BankAccountCommand{to, BankAccountCommand::deposit,
      amount}
    } {}
};
```

Here we're reuse the base class constructor to initialize the object with the two commands and then reuse the base class' `call()`/`undo()` implementations.

But wait, that's not right, is it? The base class implementations don't quite cut it because they don't incorporate the idea of failure. If I fail to withdraw money from A, I shouldn't deposit that money to B: the entire chain should cancel itself.

To support this idea, more drastic changes are required. We need to

- Add a succeeded flag to Command.

- Record the success or failure of *every* operation.

- Ensure that the command can only be undone if it originally succeeded.

- Introduce a new in-between class called DependentCompositeCommand that is very careful about actually rolling back the commands.

When calling each command, we only do so if the previous one succeeded; otherwise, we simply set the success flag to false.

```
void call() override
{
  bool ok = true;
  for (auto& cmd : *this)
  {
    if (ok)
    {
      cmd.call();
      ok = cmd.succeeded;
    }
    else
    {
      cmd.succeeded = false;
    }
  }
}
```

There is no need to override the undo() because each of our commands checks its own success flag and undoes the operation only if it's set to true. Figure 14-1 shows a visual summary.

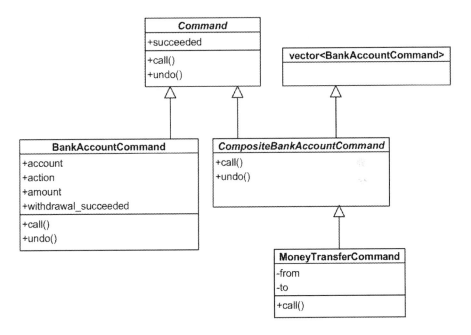

Figure 14-1. *Composite command class diagram*

One can imagine an even more restrictive mechanic where a composite command only succeeds if *all* of its parts succeed (think about a transfer where the withdrawal succeeds but the deposit fails – would you want it to go through?) – this is a bit harder to implement, and I again leave it as an exercise to the reader.

The entire purpose of this section was to illustrate how a simple Command-based approach can get quite complicated when real-world business requirements are taken into account. Whether or not you actually *need* this complexity... well, that is up to you.

Command Query Separation

The notion of Command Query Separation (CQS) is the idea that operations in a system fall broadly into the following two categories:

- Commands, which are instructions for the system to perform some operation that involves mutation of state, but yields no value

- Queries, which are requests for information that yield values but do not mutate state

Any object that presently exposes its state directly for reading and writing can hide its state (make it private) and then, instead of providing getter and setter pairs, can offer a singular interface. Here's what I mean: suppose we have a Creature with two properties called strength and agility. We can define the creature thus:

```
class Creature
{
  int strength, agility;
public:
  Creature(int strength, int agility)
    : strength{strength}, agility{agility} {}

  void process_command(const CreatureCommand& cc);
  int process_query(const CreatureQuery& q) const;
};
```

As you can see, there are no getters and setters, but we do have two (just two!) API members called process_command() and process_query() that are meant to be used for *all* interactions with Creature objects. Both

of these are dedicated classes which, together with the CreatureAbility
enumeration, are defined as follows:

```
enum class CreatureAbility { strength, agility };

struct CreatureCommand
{
  enum Action { set, increaseBy, decreaseBy } action;
  CreatureAbility ability;
  int amount;
};

struct CreatureQuery
{
  CreatureAbility ability;
};
```

As you can see, the command describes what member you want to
change and how you want to change it and by how much. The query object
only specifies what to query, and we assume that the result of the query
is returned from the function, rather than set in the query object itself (if
other objects affect this one, as we have seen already, that's how you would
do it instead).

So here is the process_command() definition:

```
void Creature::process_command(const CreatureCommand &cc)
{
  int* ability;
  switch (cc.ability)
  {
    case CreatureAbility::strength:
      ability = &strength;
      break;
```

```
    case CreatureAbility::agility:
      ability = &agility;
      break;
  }
  switch (cc.action)
  {
    case CreatureCommand::set:
      *ability = cc.amount;
      break;
    case CreatureCommand::increaseBy:
      *ability += cc.amount;
      break;
    case CreatureCommand::decreaseBy:
      *ability -= cc.amount;
      break;
  }
}
```

And here is the much simpler process_query() definition:

```
int Creature::process_query(const CreatureQuery &q) const
{
  switch (q.ability)
  {
    case CreatureAbility::strength: return strength;
    case CreatureAbility::agility: return agility;
  }
  return 0;
}
```

If you want logging or persistence of these commands and queries, you now have just two locations whether this needs to be done. The only real issue with all of this is how difficult the API is to work with for someone who just wants to manipulate the object in a familiar manner.

Luckily for us, we can always manufacture getter/setter pairs if we want to; these would just call the process_ methods with appropriate arguments:

```
void Creature::set_strength(int value)
{
  process_command(CreatureCommand{
    CreatureCommand::set, CreatureAbility::strength, value
  });
}

int Creature::get_strength() const
{
  return process_query(CreatureQuery{CreatureAbility::strength});
}
```

This is, admittedly, a very simplistic illustration of what actually happens inside systems that do CQS, but it hopefully gives an idea of how one can split *all* object interfaces into Command and Query parts.

Summary

The Command design pattern is simple: what it basically suggests is that objects can communicate with one another using special objects that encapsulate instructions, rather than specifying those same instructions as arguments to a method.

Sometimes, you don't want such an object to mutate the target or cause it to do something specific; instead, you want to use such an object to inquire a value from the target, in which case we typically call such an object a Query. While, in most cases, a query is an immutable object that relies on the return type of the method, there *are* situations (see, e.g., the Chain of Responsibility Broker Chain example) when you want the result that's being returned to be modified by other components. But the components themselves are still not modified, only the result is.

Commands are used a lot in UI systems to encapsulate typical actions (e.g., copy or paste) and then allow a single command to be invoked by several different means. For example, you can copy by using the top-level application menu, a button on the toolbar, or by pressing a keyboard shortcut. Finally, these actions can be combined into macros – sequences of actions that can be recorded and then replayed at will.

CHAPTER 15

Interpreter

The goal of the Interpreter design pattern is, as you may have guessed, to interpret input, particularly *textual* input – although, to be fair, it really doesn't matter. The notion of an Interpreter relates directly to Compiler Theory and similar courses taught at universities. Since we don't have nearly enough space here to delve into the complexities of different types of parsers and whatnot, the purpose of this chapter is to simply show some examples of the kinds of things you might want to interpret.

Here are a few fairly obvious ones:

- Numeric literals such as 42 or 1.234e12 need to be interpreted to be stored efficiently in binary. In C++, these operations are covered both via C APIs such as stof() and more sophisticated libraries such as Boost. LexicalCast.

- Regular expressions help us find patterns in text, but they are themselves a separate, embedded domain-specific language (DSL). And naturally, before using them, they must be interpreted correctly.

- Any structured data, be it CSV, XML, JSON, or something more complicated, requires interpretation before it can be used.

© Dmitri Nesteruk 2022
D. Nesteruk, *Design Patterns in Modern C++20*,
https://doi.org/10.1007/978-1-4842-7295-4_15

- At the pinnacle of the application of Interpreter, we have fully fledged programming languages. After all, a compiler or interpreter for a language like C or Python must actually understand the language before making something executable.

Given the proliferation and diversity of challenges related to interpretation, we shall simply look at some examples. These serve to illustrate how one can build an Interpreter: either by making something from scratch or by leveraging a library that helps do these things at an industrial scale.

Parsing Integral Numbers

The parsing of numbers is a key operation that is often optimized (redesigned) by developers of algorithmic trading systems. The default implementations provided by the Standard Library are very flexible and can handle many different number formats, but in real life the stock market typically feeds you data with a single uniform format (e.g., just positive integers), allowing us to trade flexibility for performance and to create much faster (orders of magnitude) parsers.

Consider a method such as atoi(). This method is very powerful: not only can it parse the string "12345" but it can do the following:

- Perform validation, returning an error value if the number doesn't parse.

- Parse numbers prefixed by zero (e.g., 007) or with a plus (e.g., +88).

- Parse numbers that have a decimal point (even if they are integers).

- Detect numbers greater than maximum or less than minimum.

A similar function, stoi(), uses exceptions so that parsing invalid data does not result in undefined behavior.

This is all well and good, but completely unnecessary if we expect data to always be valid and to fall within some predictable range (as market asset prices typically do). Consequently, we can eschew the various bells and whistles and define a function such as

```
int better_atoi(const char* str)
{
  int val{0};
  while(*str) {
    val = val*10 + (*str++ - '0');
  }
  return val;
}
```

This function offers, on my machine, a five-fold increase in performance compared to the system call. As I'm sure you'll agree, this is a very large performance increase for a zero-effort implementation!

A real-world integer parsing function, used "in anger" in an algorithmic trading system, gives sub-nanosecond performance, which implies a 25× performance improvement when compared to the standard atoi() call. For such an implementation, C++ alone is insufficient, forcing us to dive into the depth of SIMD intrinsics.

Numeric Expression Evaluator

Let's imagine that we decide to parse *very* simple mathematical expressions such as 3+(5-4), that is, we'll restrict ourselves to addition, subtraction, and round brackets. We want a program that can read such an expression and, of course, calculate the expression's final value.

We are going to build the calculator *by hand*, without resorting to any parsing framework. This should hopefully highlight *some* of the complexity involved in parsing textual input.

Lexing

The first step to interpreting an expression is called *lexing*, and it involves turning a sequence of character into a sequence of *tokens*. A token is typically a primitive syntactic element, and we should end up with a flat sequence of these. In our case, a token can be

- An integer

- An operator (plus or minus)

- An opening or closing parenthesis

Thus, we can define the following structure:

```
struct Token
{
  enum Type { integer, plus, minus, lparen, rparen } type;
  string text;

  explicit Token(Type type, const string& text)
    : type{type}, text{text} {}

  friend ostream& operator<<(ostream& os, const Token& obj)
  {
    return os << "`" << obj.text << "`";
  }
};
```

You'll note that Token is not an enum because, apart from the type, we also want to store the text that this token relates to, since it is not always predefined. In this particular case, we store the token as a string, whereas if we assume that tokens only live as long as the input does and need not be modified, we can use a string_view instead.

So now, given a string containing an expression, we can define a lexing process that will turn textual input into a vector<Token>:

```
vector<Token> lex(const string& input)
{
  vector<Token> result;

  for (int i = 0; i < input.size(); ++i)
  {
    switch (input[i])
    {
    case '+':
      result.emplace_back(Token::plus, "+");
      break;
    case '-':
      result.emplace_back(Token::minus, "-");
      break;
    case '(':
      result.emplace_back(Token::lparen, "(");
      break;
    case ')':
      result.emplace_back(Token::rparen, ")");
      break;
    default:
      // number ???
    }
  }
}
```

Parsing predefined tokens is easy. In fact, we could have added them as a

```
map<BinaryOperation::Type, char>
```

to simplify things. But parsing a number is not so easy. If we hit a 1, we should wait and see what the next character is. For this, we define a separate routine:

```
ostringstream buffer;
buffer << input[i];
for (int j = i + 1; j < input.size(); ++j)
{
  if (isdigit(input[j]))
  {
    buffer << input[j];
    ++i;
  }
  else
  {
    result.emplace_back(Token::integer, buffer.str());
    buffer.str("");
    break;
  }
}

if (auto str = buffer.str(); str.length() > 0)
  result.emplace_back(Token::integer, str);
```

Essentially, while we keep reading (pumping) digits, we add them to the buffer. When we're done, we make a Token out of the entire buffer and add it to the resulting vector – this can happen either when we encounter something that's not a number (such as a parenthesis) or once we've reached the end of input.

Parsing

The process of *parsing* turns a sequence of tokens into meaningful, typically object-oriented, structures. At the top, it's often useful to have an abstract parent type that all elements of the tree implement:

```
struct Element
{
  virtual int eval() const = 0;
};
```

The type's eval() function evaluates this element's numeric value. Next, we can create an element for storing integral values (such as 1, 5, or 42):

```
struct Integer : Element
{
  int value;

  explicit Integer(const int value)
    : value(value) {}

  int eval() const override { return value; }
};
```

If we don't have an Integer, we must have an operation such as addition or subtraction. In our case, all operations are *binary*, meaning they have two parts. For example, 2+3 in our model can be represented in pseudocode as BinaryOperation{Literal{2}, Literal{3}, addition}:

```
struct BinaryOperation : Element
{
  enum Type { addition, subtraction } type;
  shared_ptr<Element> lhs, rhs;
```

251

```
  int eval() const override
  {
    if (type == addition)
      return lhs->eval() + rhs->eval();
    return lhs->eval() - rhs->eval();
  }
};
```

Note that, in the preceding, I'm using an enum instead of an enum class so that I can write BinaryOperation::addition later on.

But anyways, on to the parsing process. All we need to do is turn a sequence of Tokens into a binary tree of Expressions. From the outset, it can look as follows:

```
shared_ptr<Element> parse(const vector<Token>& tokens)
{
  auto result = make_unique<BinaryOperation>();
  bool have_lhs = false; // this will need some explaining :)
  for (size_t i = 0; i < tokens.size(); i++)
  {
    auto token = tokens[i];
    switch(token.type)
    {
      // process each of the tokens in turn
    }
  }
  return result;
}
```

The only thing we need to discuss is the have_lhs variable. Remember, what we are trying to get is a tree, and at the *root* of that tree, we expect a BinaryExpression which, by definition, has left and right sides. But when we are on a number, how do we know if it's the left or right side of an expression? That's right, we don't, which is why we track this.

Now let's go through these case by case. First, integers – these map directly to our `Integer` construct, so all we have to do is turn text into a number. (Incidentally, we could have also done this at the lexing stage if we wanted to.)

```
case Token::integer:
{
  int value = boost::lexical_cast<int>(token.text);
  auto integer = make_shared<Integer>(value);
  if (!have_lhs) {
    result->lhs = integer;
    have_lhs = true;
  }
  else result->rhs = integer;
}
```

The `plus` and `minus` tokens simply determine the type of the operation we're currently processing, so they're easy:

```
case Token::plus:
  result->type = BinaryOperation::addition;
  break;
case Token::minus:
  result->type = BinaryOperation::subtraction;
  break;
```

And then there's the left parenthesis. Yep, just the left, we don't detect the right one explicitly. Basically, the idea here is simple: find the closing right parenthesis (I'm ignoring nested brackets for now), rip out the entire subexpression, parse() it recursively, and set as the left- or right-hand side of the expression we're currently working with:

```cpp
case Token::lparen:
{
  int j = i;
  for (; j < tokens.size(); ++j)
    if (tokens[j].type == Token::rparen)
      break; // found it!

  vector<Token> subexpression(&tokens[i + 1], &tokens[j]);
  auto element = parse(subexpression);
  if (!have_lhs)
  {
    result->lhs = element;
    have_lhs = true;
  }
  else result->rhs = element;
  i = j; // advance
}
```

In a real-world scenario, you'd want a lot more safety features in here: not just handling nested parentheses (which I think is a must), but handling incorrect expressions where the closing parenthesis is missing. If it is indeed missing, how would you handle it? Throw an exception? Try to parse whatever's left and assume the closing is at the very end? Something else? All of these issues are left as the exercise to the reader.

From experience with C++ itself, we know that making meaningful error messages for parsing errors is *very* hard. In fact, you will find a phenomenon called *skipping* where, in doubt, the lexer or parser will attempt to skip incorrect code until it meets something meaningful: precisely this approach is adopted by static analysis tools that are expected to work correctly on incomplete code as the user is typing it.

Using the Lexer and Parser

With both `lex()` and `parse()` implemented, we can finally parse the expression and calculate its value:

```
string input{ "(13-4)-(12+1)" };
auto tokens = lex(input);
auto parsed = parse(tokens);
cout << input << " = " << parsed->eval() << endl;
// prints "(13-4)-(12+1) = -4"
```

Parsing with Boost.Spirit

In the real world, unless micro-optimizations such as SIMD are involved, hardly anyone hand-rolls parsers for something complicated. Sure, if you are parsing a "trivial" data storage format such as XML or JSON, hand-rolling the parser is easy. But if you are implementing your own DSL (domain-specific language) or programming language, this is not an option.

Boost.Spirit is a library which helps the creation of parsers by providing succinct (though not particularly intuitive) APIs for the construction of parsers. The library does not attempt to explicitly separate the lexing and parsing stages (unless you really want to), allowing you to define how textual constructs get mapped onto objects of types you define.

Let me show you some examples of using Boost.Spirit with the Tlön programming language.[1]

---

[1] Tlön is a toy language that I built to demo the idea of "if you don't like existing languages, build a new one." It uses Boost.Spirit and cross-compiles (transpiles) into C++. It is open source and can be found at https://github.com/nesteruk/tlon

Abstract Syntax Tree

To start with, you need your AST (abstract syntax tree). In this respect, I simply make a base class that supports the Visitor design pattern, since traversal of these structures is very important:

```
struct ast_element
{
  virtual ~ast_element() = default;
  virtual void accept(ast_element_visitor& visitor) = 0;
};
```

This interface is then used to define different code constructs in my language, for example:

```
struct property : ast_element
{
  vector<wstring> names;
  type_specification type;
  bool is_constant{ false };
  wstring default_value;

  void accept(ast_element_visitor& visitor) override
  {
    visitor.visit(*this);
  }
};
```

This definition of a property has four different parts, each stored in a publically accessible field. Note that it uses a type_specification, which is itself another ast_element.

Every single class of an AST needs to be adapted for Boost.Fusion – another Boost library that supports a fusion (hence the name) of compile time (metaprogramming) and runtime algorithms. The adaptation code is simple enough:

```
BOOST_FUSION_ADAPT_STRUCT(
  tlön::property,
  (vector<wstring>, names),
  (tlön::type_specification, type),
  (bool, is_constant),
  (wstring, default_value)
)
```

Spirit has no trouble parsing into common data types such as an std::vector or std::optional. It does have a bit more problems with polymorphism: rather than having your AST types inherit from one another, Spirit prefers that you use a variant, that is:

```
typedef variant<function_body, property, function_signature>
class_member;
```

Parser

Boost.Spirit lets us define the parser as a set of rules. The syntax that is used is very similar to regular expressions or BNF notation, except the operators are placed *before* the symbol, not after. Here is an example rule:

```
class_declaration_rule %=
  lit(L"class ") >> +(alnum) % '.'
  >> -(lit(L"(") >> -parameter_declaration_rule % ',' >>
  lit(")"))
  >> "{"
  >> *(function_body_rule | property_rule | function_signature_rule)
  >> "}";
```

The preceding expects a class declaration to start with the word class. It then expects one or more words (each word is one or more alphanumeric characters, thus +(alnum)), separated with periods '.' – this is what the % operator is used for. The result, as you may have guessed, would map onto a vector. Subsequently, after the curly braces, we expect zero or more definitions of functions, properties, or function signatures – the fields these would be mapped to correspond to our prior definition using a variant.

Naturally, some element is the "root" of the entire hierarchy of AST elements. In our case, this root is called a file (surprise!), and here is a function that both parses the file and pretty-prints it:

```
template<typename TLanguagePrinter, typename Iterator>
wstring parse(Iterator first, Iterator last)
{
  using spirit::qi::phrase_parse;

  file f;
  file_parser<wstring::const_iterator> fp{};
  auto b = phrase_parse(first, last, fp, space, f);
  if (b)
  {
    return TLanguagePrinter{}.pretty_print(f);
  }
  return wstring(L"FAIL");
}
```

The type TLanguagePrinter is essentially a visitor that knows how to render our AST in a specific language, such as C++.

Printer

Having parsed the language, we might want to compile it or, in my case, transpile it into some other language. This is rather easy considering that we have previously implemented an accept() method into the entire AST hierarchy.

The only challenge is what to do with the variant types, because those need special visitors. In the case of std::variant, what you are after is std::visit(), but since we are using a boost::variant, the function to call for is boost::accept_visitor(). This function requires that you give it an instance of a class inheriting from static_visitor, with function call overloads for every possible type. Here's an example:

```
struct default_value_visitor : static_visitor<>
{
  cpp_printer& printer;

  explicit default_value_visitor(cpp_printer& printer)
    : printer{printer} {}

  void operator()(const basic_type& bt) const
  {
    // for a scalar value, we just dump its default
    printer.buffer << printer.default_value_for(bt.name);
  }

  void operator()(const tuple_signature& ts) const
  {
    for (auto& e : ts.elements)
    {
      this->operator()(e.type);
      printer.buffer << ", ";
    }
```

```
    printer.backtrack(2);
  }
};
```

You would then call `accept_visitor(foo, default_value_visitor{...})` and the correct overload will be called depending on the type of object actually stored in the `variant`.

Summary

Comparatively speaking, the Interpreter design pattern is somewhat uncommon – the challenges of building parsers is nowadays considered inessential, which is why I see it being removed from Computer Science courses in many universities. Also, unless you plan to work in language design or, say, making tools for static code analysis, you are unlikely to find the skills in building parsers in high demand.

That said, the challenge of interpretation is a whole separate field of Computer Science that a single chapter of a Design Patterns book cannot reasonably do justice to. If you are interested in the subject, I recommend you check out frameworks such as Lex/Yacc, ANTLR, and many others that are specifically geared for lexer/parser construction. I can also recommend writing static analysis plug-ins for popular IDEs – this is a great way to get a feel for how real ASTs look and how they are traversed and modified.

CHAPTER 16

Iterator

Whenever you start working with complicated data structures, you encounter the problem of *traversal*. This can be handled in different ways, but the most common way of traversing, say, a vector is using something called an *iterator*.

An iterator is, quite simply, an object that can point to an element of a collection and also knows how to move to the next element in the collection. As such, it is only required to implement the ++ operator and the != operator (so you can compare two iterators and check if they point to the same thing). That's it.

The C++ Standard Library makes heavy use of iterators, so we shall discuss the way they are used there, and then we'll take a look at how to make our own iterators and what the limitations of iterators are.

Iterators in the Standard Library

Imagine you have a list of names such as

```
vector<string> names{ "john", "jane", "jill", "jack" };
```

If you want to get the first name in the names collection, you call a function called begin(). This function doesn't give you the first name by value or by reference; instead, it gives you an iterator:

```
vector<string>::iterator it = names.begin(); // begin(names)
```

© Dmitri Nesteruk 2022
D. Nesteruk, *Design Patterns in Modern C++20*,
https://doi.org/10.1007/978-1-4842-7295-4_16

The function `begin()` exists as both a member function of `vector` and a global function. The global one is particularly useful for arrays (C-style arrays, not `std::array`) because they cannot have member functions.

So `begin()` returns an iterator which you can think of as a pointer: in the case of a `vector`, it has similar mechanics. For example, you can dereference the iterator to print the actual name:

```
cout << "first name is " << *it << "\n";
// first name is john
```

The iterator that we are given knows how to *advance*, that is, move to point to the next element. It's important to realize that the ++ refers to the idea of moving forward, that is, it is *not* the same as a ++ for pointers where you increase a memory address.

```
++it; // now points to jane
```

We can also use the iterator (same way as a pointer) to modify the element it points to:

```
it->append(" goodall"s);
cout << "second name is " << *it << "\n";
// second name is jane goodall
```

Now, the counterpart to `begin()` is, of course, `end()`, but it doesn't point to the last element – instead, it points to the element *after* the last one. Here's a clumsy illustration:

```
      1 2 3 4
 begin() ^        ^ end()
```

You can use end() as the terminating condition. For example, let's print the rest of those names using our it iterator variable:

```
while (++it != names.end())
{
  cout << "another name: " << *it << "\n";
}
// another name: jill
// another name: jack
```

In addition to begin() and end(), we also have rbegin() and rend() which allow us to move backward through the collection. In this case, as you may have guessed, rbegin() points to the last element and rend() to one before the first.

```
for (auto ri = rbegin(names); ri != rend(names); ++ri)
{
  cout << *ri;
  if (ri + 1 != rend(names)) // iterator arithmetic
    cout << ", ";
}
cout << endl;
// jack, jill, jane goodall, john
```

There are two things worth pointing out here. First, even though we are going through the vector backward, we still use the ++ operator on the iterator. Second, we are allowed to do arithmetic: again, when I write ri + 1, this refers to the element *just before* ri and not after.

We can also have constant iterators which do not allow modification of the object: they are returned through cbegin()/cend() and, of course, there are reverse varieties crbegin()/crend() too:

```
vector<string>::const_reverse_iterator jack = crbegin(names);
// won't work
*jack += " reacher";
```

Finally, it's worth mentioning the Modern C++ gem, a *range-based for loop* that serves as a shorthand for iterating all the way from a container's begin() until we reach its end():

```
for (auto& name : names)
  cout << "name = " << name << "\n";
```

Notice that the iterator is automatically dereferenced here: the variable name is a reference, but you could equally iterate by value.

Traversing a Binary Tree

Let's go through the classic Computer Science exercise of traversing a binary tree. First of all, we shall define a node of this tree as follows:

```
template <typename T> struct Node
{
  T value;
  Node<T> *left{nullptr};
  Node<T> *right{nullptr};
  Node<T> *parent{nullptr};
  BinaryTree<T>* tree{nullptr};
};
```

Each node has a pointer to its `left` and `right` branches, its parent (if it has one), and also to the entire tree. A node can be constructed either on its own or with a specification of its children:

```
explicit Node(const T& value)
  : value(value) {}

Node(const T& value, Node<T>* const left, Node<T>* const right)
    : value{value}, left{left}, right{right}
{
  this->left->tree = this->right->tree = tree;
  this->left->parent = this->right->parent = this;
}
```

Finally, we introduce a utility member function to set the `tree` pointer. This is done recursively across all of the `Node`'s children:

```
void set_tree(BinaryTree<T>* t)
{
  tree = t;
  if (left) left->set_tree(t);
  if (right) right->set_tree(t);
}
```

Armed with this, we can now define a structure called `BinaryTree` – it is precisely this structure that will permit iteration.

```
template <typename T> struct BinaryTree
{
  Node<T>* root = nullptr;

  explicit BinaryTree(Node<T>* const root)
    : root{ root }
```

```
  {
    root->set_tree(this);
  }
};
```

Now we can define an iterator for the tree. There are three common ways of iterating a binary tree, and the one we'll implement first is pre-order:

- We return the element as soon as it is encountered.

- We recursively traverse the left subtree.

- We recursively traverse the right subtree.

So let's start with a constructor:

```
template <typename U>
struct PreOrderIterator
{
  Node<U>* current;

  explicit PreOrderIterator(Node<U>* current)
    : current{current} {}

  // other members here
};
```

We need to define operator != to compare with other iterators. Since our iterator acts as a pointer, this is trivial:

```
bool operator!=(const PreOrderIterator<U>& other)
{
  return current != other.current;
}
```

We also need the * operator for dereferencing:

```
Node<U>& operator*() { return *current; }
```

Now, here comes the hard part: traversing the tree. The challenge here is that we cannot make the algorithm recursive – remember, traversal happens in the ++ operator, so we end up implementing it as follows:

```
PreOrderIterator<U>& operator++()
{
  if (current->right)
  {
    current = current->right;
    while (current->left)
      current = current->left;
  }
  else
  {
    Node<T>* p = current->parent;
    while (p && current == p->right)
    {
      current = p;
      p = p->parent;
    }
    current = p;
  }
  return *this;
}
```

This is quite messy! Furthermore, it looks nothing like the classic implementation of tree traversal you'd find on Wikipedia, precisely because we don't have recursion available to us. We'll get back to this in a while.

Now, the final question is how to expose the iterator from our BinaryTree. If we were to define it as the *default* iterator for the tree, we could populate its members as follows:

```
typedef PreOrderIterator<T> iterator;

iterator begin()
{
  Node<T>* n = root;

  if (n)
    while (n->left)
      n = n->left;
  return iterator{ n };
}

iterator end()
{
  return iterator{ nullptr };
}
```

It's worth noting that, in begin(), iteration doesn't start from the root of the entire tree; instead, it starts from the leftmost available node.

Now that all the pieces are in place, here is how we would do the traversal:

```
BinaryTree<string> family{
  new Node<string>{"me",
    new Node<string>{"mother",
      new Node<string>{"mother's mother"},
      new Node<string>{"mother's father"}
    },
    new Node<string>{"father"}
  }
};
```

```
for (auto it = family.begin(); it != family.end(); ++it)
{
  cout << (*it)->value << "\n";
}
```

You could also expose this form of traversal as a separate object, that is:

```
class pre_order_traversal
{
  BinaryTree<T>& tree;
public:
  pre_order_traversal(BinaryTree<T>& tree) : tree{tree} {}
  iterator begin() { return tree.begin(); }
  iterator end() { return tree.end(); }
} pre_order;
```

to be used as

```
for (const auto& it: family.pre_order)
{
  cout << it.value << "\n";
}
```

Similarly, one could define in_order and post_order traversal algorithms to expose appropriate iterators.

Iteration with Coroutines

In our traversal code, operator++ is, sadly, an unreadable mess that doesn't match anything you'd read about tree traversal on Wikipedia.[1] Our code works, but it only works because we pre-initialize the iterator to start

---

[1] https://en.wikipedia.org/wiki/Tree_traversal

at the leftmost node instead of the root node, which is also a rather strange thing to do.

This problem exists because the ++ operator function is not resumable: it cannot keep its stack between calls, and, as a result, recursion is impossible. Now, what if we had a mechanism to have our cake and eat it too: resumable functions that can perform proper recursion? Well, that's exactly what *coroutines* are for.

Coroutines are a C++20 feature. The support for coroutines lives in the <coroutine> header, but the support for generators is currently not part of the Standard Library. Consequently, you would either need to find an implementation or to check whether your compiler ships with an implementation already. For example, when using MSVC, and implementation of the generator<T> type can be found in the <experimental/generator> header.

With coroutines, we can implement post-order tree traversal as follows:

```cpp
generator<Node<T>*> post_order_impl(Node<T>* node) const
{
  if (node)
  {
    for (auto x : post_order_impl(node->left))
      co_yield x;
    for (auto y : post_order_impl(node->right))
      co_yield y;

    co_yield node;
  }
}

generator<Node<T>*> post_order() const
{
  return post_order_impl(root);
}
```

Isn't this great? The algorithm is finally readable again! Furthermore, there's no begin()/end() in sight: we simply return a generator, which is a type specifically designed to progressively return values that are fed to it with co_yield. After each of the values is yielded, we can suspend execution and do something else (say, print the value), and then resume the iteration without losing the context. This is what makes recursion possible and allows us to write this:

```
for (auto it: family.post_order())
{
  cout << it->value << endl;
}
```

Coroutines are the future of C++ and solve lots of problems for which conventional iterators are either ugly or unsuitable.

Summary

The Iterator design pattern is omnipresent in C++ in both explicit and implicit (e.g., range-based for) forms. Different types of iterators exist for iterating different objects: for example, reverse iterators might apply to a vector, but not to a singly linked list.

Implementing your own iterator is as simple as providing the ++ and != operators. Most iterators are simply pointer façades and are meant to be used to traverse the collection once before they are thrown away.

Coroutines fix some of the issues present in iterators: they allow state to be preserved between calls – something that other languages (e.g., C#) have implemented a long time ago. As a consequence, coroutines allow us to write recursive algorithms that need to yield values one after another and preserve the position of the iterator between the calls.

CHAPTER 17

Mediator

A large proportion of the code we write has different components (classes) that communicate with one another through direct references or pointers. However, there are situations when you don't want objects to be aware of each other's presence. Or, perhaps you *do* want them to be aware of one another, but you still don't want them to communicate through pointers or references because those can go stale and the last thing you want is to dereference a `nullptr`.

The Mediator design pattern is a mechanism for facilitating communication between the components. Naturally, the mediator itself needs to be accessible by every component taking part, which means it should either be a global `static` variable or, alternatively, just a reference that gets injected into every component.

Chat Room

Your typical Internet chat room is the classic example of the Mediator design pattern, so let's implement it before we move on to the more complicated examples.

The most trivial implementation of a participant in a chat room can be as simple as

```
struct Person
{
```

```
  string name;
  ChatRoom* room{nullptr};
  vector<string> chat_log;

  Person(const string& name);

  void receive(const string& origin, const string& message);
  void say(const string& message) const;
  void pm(const string& who, const string& message) const;
};
```

What we have is a person that has a name (user id), a chat log, and a pointer to the ChatRoom they are in. We have a constructor and three member functions, specifically:

- receive() allows us to receive a message. Typically, what this function would do is show the message on the user's screen and also add it to their chat log. Note that different users can have very different chat logs.

- say() allows the person to broadcast a message to everyone in the room.

- pm() is private messaging functionality. You need to specify the name of the person the message is intended for.

Both say() and pm() just relay operations to the chat room. Speaking of which, let's actually implement ChatRoom – it's not particularly complicated:

```
struct ChatRoom
{
  vector<Person*> people; // assume append-only

  void join(Person* p);
```

```
  void broadcast(const string& origin, const string& message);
  void message(const string& origin, const string& who,
    const string& message);
};
```

Whether to use pointers, references, or, say, a shared_ptr for actually storing a list of chat room participants is ultimately up to you: the only restriction is that a vector<> cannot store references. I have decided to go with pointers here. The ChatRoom API is very simple:

- join() gets a person to join the room. We are not going to implement leave(), instead deferring the idea to a subsequent example in this chapter.

- broadcast() sends the message to everyone except, of course, the person that sent it in the first place.

- message() sends a private message.

The implementation of join() is as follows:

```
void ChatRoom::join(Person* p)
{
  string join_msg = p->name + " joins the chat";
  broadcast("room", join_msg);
  p->room = this;
  people.push_back(p);
}
```

Just like a classic IRC chat room, we broadcast the message that someone has joined to everyone in the room. The origin in this case is specified as "room" rather than the person that's joined. We then set the person's room pointer and add them to the list of people in the room.

Now, let's look at the broadcast() member function. This is where a message is sent to every room participant. Remember, each participant has its own Person::receive() function for processing the message, so the implementation is somewhat trivial:

```
void ChatRoom::broadcast(const string& origin, const string&
message)
{
  for (auto p : people)
    if (p->name != origin)
      p->receive(origin, message);
}
```

Whether or not we want to prevent a broadcast message to be relayed to ourselves is a point of debate, but I'm actively avoiding it here. Everyone else gets the message, though.

Finally, here is private messaging implemented with message():

```
void ChatRoom::message(const string& origin,
  const string& who, const string& message)
{
  auto target = find_if(begin(people), end(people),
    [&](const Person* p) { return p->name == who; });
  if (target != end(people))
  {
    (*target)->receive(origin, message);
  }
}
```

This searches for the recipient in the list of people and, if the recipient is found (because who knows, they could have left the room), dispatches the message to that person.

Coming back to Person's implementations of say() and pm(), here they are:

```
void Person::say(const string& message) const
{
  room->broadcast(name, message);
}

void Person::pm(const string& who, const string& message) const
{
  room->message(name, who, message);
}
```

As for receive(), well, this is a good place to actually display the message on screen as well as add it to the chat log.

```
void Person::receive(const string& origin, const string&
message)
{
  string s{ origin + ": \"" + message + "\"" };
  cout << "[" << name << "'s chat session] " << s << "\n";
  chat_log.emplace_back(s);
}
```

We go the extra mile here by displaying not just who the message came from but whose chat session we're currently in – this will be useful for diagnosing who said what and when.

Here is the scenario that we'll run through:

```
ChatRoom room;

Person john{ "john" };
Person jane{ "jane" };
room.join(&john);
room.join(&jane);
```

```
john.say("hi room");
jane.say("oh, hey john");

Person simon("simon");
room.join(&simon);
simon.say("hi everyone!");

jane.pm("simon", "glad you could join us, simon");
```

Here is the output the program produces:

```
[john's chat session] room: "jane joins the chat"
[jane's chat session] john: "hi room"
[john's chat session] jane: "oh, hey john"
[john's chat session] room: "simon joins the chat"
[jane's chat session] room: "simon joins the chat"
[john's chat session] simon: "hi everyone!"
[jane's chat session] simon: "hi everyone!"
[simon's chat session] jane: "glad you could join us, simon"
```

See Figure 17-1 for a visual illustration of the calls involved in this chat session.

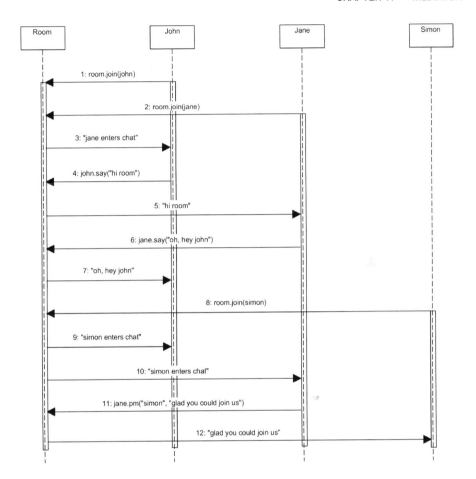

Figure 17-1. *Visualized chat session*

Mediator with Events

In the chat room example, we've encountered a consistent theme: the participants need notification whenever someone posts a message. This seems like a perfect scenario for the Observer pattern, which is discussed later in the book: the idea of the mediator having an event that is shared by all participants; participants can then subscribe to the event to receive notifications, and they can also cause the event to fire, thus triggering said notifications.

Events are not built into C++ (unlike, e.g., C#), so we'll use a library solution for this demo. Boost.Signals2 offers us the requisite functionality, albeit with a slightly different terminology: we typically speak of *signals* (objects which generate a notification) and *slots* (functions that handle notifications).

Instead of redoing the chat room once again, let's go for a simpler example: imagine a game of football (soccer) with players and a football coach. When the coach sees their team scoring, they naturally want to congratulate the player. Of course, they need some information about the event, like *who* scored the goal and how many goals they have scored so far.

We can introduce a base class for any sort of event data:

```
struct EventData
{
  virtual ~EventData() = default;
  virtual void print() const = 0;
};
```

I've added the print() function so that each event can be printed to the command line and also a virtual destructor to make ReSharper shut up about it. Now, we can derive from this class in order to store some goal-related data:

```
struct PlayerScoredData : EventData
{
  string player_name;
  int goals_scored_so_far;

  PlayerScoredData(const string& player_name,
    const int goals_scored_so_far)
    : player_name(player_name),
      goals_scored_so_far(goals_scored_so_far) {}
```

```
  void print() const override
  {
    cout << player_name << " has scored! (their "
      << goals_scored_so_far << " goal)" << "\n";
  }
};
```

We are once again going to build a mediator, but it will have *no* behaviors! With an event-driven infrastructure, they are no longer needed:

```
struct Game
{
  signal<void(EventData*)> events; // observer
};
```

In fact, you could get away with just having a global signal variable and not make a Game class at all, but we are using the principle of least surprise here, and if a Game& is injected into a component, we know there's a clear dependency there.

We can now construct the Player class. A player has a name, the number of goals they scored during the match, and a reference to the mediator Game, of course:

```
struct Player
{
  string name;
  int goals_scored = 0;
  Game& game;

  Player(const string& name, Game& game)
    : name(name), game(game) {}

  void score()
  {
```

```
    goals_scored++;
    PlayerScoredData ps{name, goals_scored};
    game.events(&ps);
  }
};
```

The `Player::score()` is the interesting function here: it uses the events signal to create a `PlayerScoredData` and post it for all subscribers to see. Who gets this event? Why, a `Coach`, of course:

```
struct Coach
{
  Game& game;
  explicit Coach(Game& game) : game(game)
  {
    // celebrate if player has scored <3 goals
    game.events.connect([](EventData* e)
    {
      PlayerScoredData* ps = dynamic_
      cast<PlayerScoredData*>(e);
      if (ps && ps->goals_scored_so_far < 3)
      {
        cout << "coach says: well done, " << ps->player_name
          << "\n";
      }
    });
  }
};
```

The implementation of the `Coach` class is simple; our coach doesn't even get a name. But we do give them a constructor where a subscription is created to game.events such that, whenever something happens, the coach gets to process the event data in the provided lambda (slot).

Notice that the argument type of the lambda is EventData* – we don't know if a player has scored or has been sent off, so we need dynamic_cast (or a similar mechanism) to determine we've got the right type.

The interesting thing is that all the magic happens at the set-up stage: there's no need to explicitly enlist slots for a particular signal. The client is free to create objects using their constructors and then, when the player scores, the notifications are sent:

```
Game game;
Player player{ "Sam", game };
Coach coach{ game };

player.score();
player.score();
player.score(); // ignored by coach
```

This produces the following output:

```
coach says: well done, Sam
coach says: well done, Sam
```

The output is only two lines long because, on the third goal, the coach isn't impressed anymore.

Service Bus As Mediator

Both of our discussions of Mediator have centered on what are essentially synchronous implementations: as one component generates some sort of event, another component on that same thread of execution gets to process it. This isn't quite how it works in the real world. For example, in a chat room, the chat room participants are on different corners of the world, whereas the chat room itself is hosted on some central server. The participants send messages and receive replies asynchronously and in separate processes.

In practice, what you have is a form of bidirectional communication that leverages much more functionality than the programming language alone provides. In the case of general-purpose communication on the Internet, for example, this might happen through the use of WebSockets, a mechanism for providing full-duplex (i.e., two-way) communication channels over a TCP connection. In the case of a corporate message exchange system, a mediator would leverage whatever underlying technology is used to send messages: something like Microsoft Message Queuing (MSMQ), Azure Service Bus, or something similar.

As soon as these forms of communication become asynchronous, we end up encountering yet another problem: how do we know that a message has been delivered? In our synchronous call example, we could have certainty, but in a set-up where you fire off a message, you need a mechanism that ensures *durability*: in other words, you need to ensure that, even in the case of a power outage that takes out some participant, the message still persists somewhere and gets to stick around until whoever is meant to process it is back online. This is ensured by separate mechanisms such as Transactional Message Queuing.

Of course, sometimes you simply do not care. You fire off messages into the abyss and, if they're lost, well, that's just tough luck.

Summary

The Mediator design pattern essentially proposes an introduction of an in-between component that everyone in a system has a reference to and can use to communicate with one another. Instead of direct memory addresses, communication can happen through identifiers (usernames, unique IDs, etc.).

The simplest implementation of a mediator is a member list and a function that goes through the list and does what it's intended to do – whether on every element of the list or selectively.

A more sophisticated implementation of Mediator can use events to allow participants to subscribe (and unsubscribe) to things happening in the system. This way, messages sent from one component to another can be treated as events. In this set-up, it is also easy for participants to unsubscribe to certain events if they are no longer interested in them, or if they are about to leave the system altogether.

CHAPTER 18

Memento

When we looked at the Command design pattern, we noted that recording a list of every single change theoretically allows you to roll back the system to any point in time – after all, you've kept a record of all the modifications.

Sometimes, though, you don't really care about playing back the state of the system, but you *do* care about being able to roll back the system to a *particular* state, if need be.

This is precisely what the Memento pattern does: it stores the state of the system and returns it as a dedicated, read-only object with no behavior of its own. This "token," if you will, can be used only for feeding it back into the system to restore it to the state it represents.

Bank Account

Let's use an example of a bank account that we've made before:

```cpp
class BankAccount
{
  const int balance = 0;
public:
  explicit BankAccount(const int balance)
    : balance(balance) {}
```

© Dmitri Nesteruk 2022
D. Nesteruk, *Design Patterns in Modern C++20*,
https://doi.org/10.1007/978-1-4842-7295-4_18

This time, we decide to make a bank account with only a deposit()
method. Instead of it being void as in previous examples, deposit() will
now be made to return a Memento:

```
Memento deposit(int amount)
{
  balance += amount;
  return { balance };
}
```

and the Memento will then be usable for rolling back the account to the
previous state:

```
void restore(const Memento& m)
{
  balance = m.balance;
}
```

As for the memento itself, we can go for a trivial implementation:

```
class Memento final
{
  int balance;
public:
  Memento(int balance)
    : balance(balance) {}
  friend class BankAccount;
};
```

There are two things to point out here:

- The Memento class is immutable. Imagine if you *could*,
  in fact, change the balance: you could roll back the
  account to a state it was never in!

- The memento declares BankAccount as a friend class. This allows the account to use the balance field. An alternative that would also have worked is to make Memento an inner class of BankAccount.

And here is how one would go about using such a set-up:

```
void memento()
{
  BankAccount ba{ 100 };
  auto m1 = ba.deposit(50);
  auto m2 = ba.deposit(25);
  cout << ba << "\n"; // Balance: 175

  // undo to m1
  ba.restore(m1);
  cout << ba << "\n"; // Balance: 150

  // redo
  ba.restore(m2);
  cout << ba << "\n"; // Balance: 175
}
```

This implementation is good enough, though there are some things missing. For example, you never get a Memento representing the opening balance because a constructor cannot return a value. You could stick a pointer in there, but it seems a bit ugly.

Undo and Redo

What if you were to store *every* Memento generated by BankAccount? In this case, you'd have a situation similar to our implementation of the Command pattern, where undo and redo operations are a byproduct of this recording. Let's see how we can get undo/redo functionality with a Memento.

We'll introduce a new bank account class, BankAccount2, that's going to keep hold of every single Memento it ever generates:

```
class BankAccount2 // supports undo/redo
{
  int balance = 0;
  vector<shared_ptr<Memento>> changes;
  int current;
public:
  explicit BankAccount2(const int balance) : balance(balance)
  {
    changes.emplace_back(make_shared<Memento>(balance));
    current = 0;
  }
```

We have now solved the problem of returning to the initial balance: the memento for the initial change is stored as well. Of course, this memento isn't actually returned, so in order to roll back to it, well, I suppose you could implement some reset() function or something – totally up to you.

In the preceding code, we are using shared_ptr to store the mementos, and we also use shared_ptr to return them. Furthermore, we are using the current field as a "pointer" into the list of changes, so that if we do decide to undo and move back a step, we can always redo and revert to something we just had.

Now, here's the implementation of the deposit() function:

```
shared_ptr<Memento> deposit(int amount)
{
  balance += amount;
  auto m = make_shared<Memento>(balance);
  changes.push_back(m);
  ++current;
```

```
  return m;
}
```

Now here comes the fun stuff (we're still listing members of BankAccount2, by the way). We add a method to restore the account state based on a memento:

```
void restore(const shared_ptr<Memento>& m)
{
  if (m)
  {
    balance = m->balance;
    changes.push_back(m);
    current = changes.size() - 1;
  }
}
```

The restoration process is significantly different to the one we've looked at earlier. First, we actually check that the shared_ptr is initialized – this is relevant because we now have a way of signaling no-ops: just return a default value. Also, when we restore a memento, we actually push that memento into the list of changes so an undo operation will work correctly on it.

Now, here is the (rather tricky) implementation of undo():

```
shared_ptr<Memento> undo()
{
  if (current > 0)
  {
    --current;
    auto m = changes[current];
    balance = m->balance;
```

```
    return m;
  }
  return{};
}
```

We can only undo() if the current pointer is greater than zero. If that's the case, we move the pointer back, grab the change at that position, apply it, and then return that change. If we cannot roll back to a previous memento, we return a default-constructed shared_ptr, for which we check in restore().

The implementation of redo() is very similar:

```
shared_ptr<Memento> redo()
{
  if (current + 1 < changes.size())
  {
    ++current;
    auto m = changes[current];
    balance = m->balance;
    return m;
  }
  return{};
}
```

Again, we need to be able to redo something: if we can, we do it safely, if not – we do nothing and return an empty pointer. Putting it all together, we can now start using the undo/redo functionality:

```
BankAccount2 ba{ 100 };
ba.deposit(50);
ba.deposit(25); // balance = 175
cout << ba << "\n";

ba.undo();
cout << "Undo 1: " << ba << "\n"; // Undo 1: 150
```

```
ba.undo();
cout << "Undo 2: " << ba << "\n"; // Undo 2: 100
ba.redo();
cout << "Redo 2: " << ba << "\n"; // Redo 2: 150
ba.undo(); // back to 100 again
```

Memory Considerations

Our simplified example demonstrates the idea of saving only one variable: the account balance. In the real world, an object could have a multitude of states, such that memory considerations would come into play when storing a possibly infinite set of object snapshots.

One very simple idea is to replace the vector with a circular buffer of limited size. For example, the following member declaration will store only the five latest changes to the account, and when a subsequent change arrives, it will simply overwrite the oldest:

```
class BankAccount3 // limited undo/redo
{
  boost::circular_buffer<shared_ptr<Memento>> changes{5};
  // as before
};
```

Curiously, when using smart pointers, this approach will not interfere with a client's ability to restore an account to any earlier state, even a state that is no longer stored in the account's finite-sized buffer.

Using Memento for Interop

If you are interested in using C++ libraries from a different programming language, the easiest solution is to expose global C/C++ functions from a dynamic library and then invoke these functions using a suitable bridging technology such as Java Native Interface (JNI) or .NET Platform Invocation Services (P/Invoke).

This isn't really a problem if you want to pass simple bits of data, such as numbers or arrays, back and forth. For example, .NET has functionality for pinning[1] an array and sending it to the "native" side for processing. It works fine, most of the time.

Problems arise when you allocate an object-oriented construct (i.e., a class) inside a C++ library and want to return this object to the caller. This isn't straightforward, because there is no universal protocol for passing native-code OOP structures between languages.[2] Apart from truly exotic solutions such as using bridging languages (e.g., Microsoft's Managed C++, which is a C++ variant that has .NET support), this problem is typically handled by serializing (encoding) all the data on one side and then unpacking it on the other side. There are many ways of doing this, including simple ones such as serializing data as XML or JSON or complicated, industry-grade solutions such as Google's Protocol Buffers.[3]

In some cases, though, you don't really need to return the full object itself. Instead, you simply want to return a handle so that this handle can be subsequently used on the C/C++ side again. You don't even need

---

[1] In .NET, objects can be relocated, so an object's memory address can change. Pinning ensures the object stays in place in memory, so its address can be taken and used in native code.

[2] On the .NET side of things, the Common Language Specification (.NET CLS) is an example of exactly such a requirement that allows all .NET-supporting languages to interoperate through a set of commonly supported data types.

[3] Protocol Buffers currently support C++, C#, Java, Python, and many other languages. See https://developers.google.com/protocol-buffers for details.

the extra memory traffic passing objects back and forth. There are many reasons why you'd want to do this, but the main reason is that you want only one side to manage the object's lifetime, since managing it on both sides is a nightmare that nobody really needs.

What you do in this case is you return a Memento. This can be anything – a string identifier, an integer, a globally unique identifier (GUID) – anything that lets you refer to the object later on. The receiving side then holds on to the token and uses that token to tell the native code when some operations on the underlying object are required.

This approach introduces an issue with lifetime management. Suppose we want the underlying object to live for as long as we have the token. How can we implement this? Well, this would mean that, on the C++ side, the token lives forever, whereas on the other side, we adorn it in a special construct (e.g., IDisposable in .NET) that has a destructor (or equivalent) function sending a message back to the C++ side that the token has been destroyed. But what if we copy the token and have two or more instances of it? Then we end up having to build a reference-counted system for tokens: something that is quite possible, but introduces extra complexity in our system.

There is also a symmetric problem: what if the C++ side has destroyed the object that the token represents? This can happen explicitly or behind the scenes when, for example, a smart pointer is used. If we try to use the corresponding token, additional checks need to be made to ensure the token is actually valid, and some sort of meaningful return value needs to be given to the native call in order to tell the other side that the token has gone stale. Again, this is extra work.

Summary

The Memento pattern is all about handing out tokens that can be used to restore the system to a prior state. Typically, the token contains all the information necessary to move the system to a particular state, and if it's small enough, you can also use it to record *all* the states of the system so as to allow not just the arbitrary resetting of the system to a prior state, but controlled navigation backward (undo) and forward (redo) of all the states the system was in.

CHAPTER 19

Null Object

We don't always choose the interfaces we work with. For example, I'd rather have my car drive me to my destination by itself, without me having to give 100% of my attention to the road and the dangerous lunatics driving next to me. And it's the same with software: sometimes you don't really want a piece of functionality, but it's built in as part of interface requirements. This means you have to provide some value even if you don't need this particular piece of functionality.

So what do you do? You make a Null Object.

Scenario

Suppose you inherited a library that uses the following interface:

```cpp
struct Logger
{
  virtual ~Logger() = default;
  virtual void info(const string& s) = 0;
  virtual void warn(const string& s) = 0;
};
```

© Dmitri Nesteruk 2022
D. Nesteruk, *Design Patterns in Modern C++20*,
https://doi.org/10.1007/978-1-4842-7295-4_19

This interface is used in bank account operations:

```cpp
class BankAccount
{
  shared_ptr<Logger> log;
public:
  string name;
  int balance = 0;

  BankAccount(const shared_ptr<Logger>& logger,
    const string& name, int balance)
    : log{logger}, name{name}, balance{balance}  {  }

  // more members here
};
```

In fact, BankAccount can have member functions similar to

```cpp
void BankAccount::deposit(int amount)
{
  balance += amount;
  log->info("Deposited $" + to_string(amount)
    + " to " + name + ", balance is now $" + to_string(balance));
}
```

So, what's the problem here? Well, if you *do* need logging, there's no problem, you just implement your own logging class

```cpp
struct ConsoleLogger : Logger
{
  void info(const string& s) override
  {
    cout << "INFO: " << s << endl;
  }
```

```
  void warn(const string& s) override
  {
    cout << "WARNING!!! " << s << endl;
  }
};
```

and you can use it straightaway. But what if you *don't want logging at all*? This is where you need a Null Object.

Null Object

Look at BankAccount's constructor once again:

```
BankAccount(const shared_ptr<Logger>& logger,
  const string& name, int balance)
```

Since the constructor takes a logger, it is *unsafe* to assume that you can get away with just passing it an uninitialized shared_ptr<BankAccount>. BankAccount *could* be checking the pointer internally before dispatching on it, but you don't know that it does, and without extra documentation it's impossible to tell.

As a consequence, the only thing that would be reasonable to pass into BankAccount is a Null Object – a class which conforms to the interface but contains no functionality:

```
struct NullLogger final : Logger
{
  void info(const string& s) override {}
  void warn(const string& s) override {}
};
```

Now, you can make an instance of NullLogger using make_shared and pass it to every component that is expecting a shared_ptr<Logger> reference. Furthermore, if you are using dependency injection, you can ensure this value gets injected into the right places automatically.

Naturally, it makes sense for a Null Object to be a Singleton too, since such an object is, in most cases, stateless. You can either explicitly turn it into a singleton (see the Singleton chapter) or simply configure the component to be a singleton in your DI container.

It's worth noting that this approach has limitations when it comes to functions that return values or manipulate internal state. For example, if either of the calls returns a bool success flag, the Null Object implementation would probably deterministically return a value of true just to be safe. But, in more complicated scenarios, there might not be a predictable way of making a Null Object that ensures consistency when interacting with its consumer.

shared_ptr Is *Not* a Null Object

It's important to note that shared_ptr and other smart pointer classes are *not* null objects themselves. A null object is something that preserves correct operation (does a no-op). But invocations on an uninitialized smart pointers crash and burn:

```
shared_ptr<int> n;
int x = *n + 1; // ouch!
```

What's interesting to note is that there is no way of making smart pointers "safe" from the perspective of invocation. In other words, you cannot write such a smart pointer where foo->bar() would magically become a no-op if foo is uninitialized. The reason for this is both the prefix * and postfix -> operators simply proxy the underlying (raw) pointer over. And there's no way of doing a no-op on a pointer member function call.

Design Improvements

Stop and think for a moment: if BankAccount was under your control, could you improve the interface such that it is easier to use? Well, here are some ideas:

- Put pointer checks everywhere. This sorts out the correctness on the BankAccount's end but doesn't stop getting library users confused. Remember, you're still not communicating that the pointer can be null.

- Add a default argument value, something like const shared_ptr<Logger>& logger = no_logging where no_logging is, say, some member of the BankAccount class. Even if this is the case, you would still have to perform checks on the pointer value in every location where you want to use the object.

- Use the optional type. This is idiomatically correct and communicates intent but leads to the horror of passing in an optional<shared_ptr<T>> and the subsequent check of whether an optional is empty or not.

Implicit Null Object

There's another radical idea which involves a double hop around the Logger interface. It involves subdividing the process of logging into invocation (we want a nice Logger interface) and operation (what the logger actually does). So, consider the following:

```
struct OptionalLogger : Logger
{
  shared_ptr<Logger> impl;
  static shared_ptr<Logger> no_logging;
```

```cpp
Logger(const shared_ptr<Logger>& logger) : impl{logger} {}

virtual void info(const string& s) override {
  if (impl) impl->info(s); // null check here
}
// and similar checks for other members
};
```

```cpp
// a static instance of a null object
shared_ptr<Logger> BankAccount::no_logging{};
```

So now we've abstracted away invocation from implementation. What we do now is redefine the `BankAccount` constructor as follows:

```cpp
shared_ptr<OptionalLogger> logger;
BankAccount(const string& name, int balance,
  const shared_ptr<Logger>& logger = no_logging)
  : log{make_shared<OptionalLogger>(logger)},
    name{name},
    balance{balance} { }
```

As you can see, there's clever subterfuge here: we are taking a `Logger` but storing an `OptionalLogger` wrapper (this is the Virtual Proxy design pattern – see Chapter 12, "Proxy"). Now, all the calls to this optional logger are safe – they only "happen" if the underlying object is available:

```cpp
BankAccount account{ "primary account", 1000 };
account.deposit(2000); // no crash
```

The proxy object that we implemented is essentially a customized version of the Pimpl idiom with built-in `nullptr` checks.

Interaction with Other Patterns

The Null Object can also appear together with a number of other design patterns. We've mentioned previously that a Null Object is a good fit for the Singleton pattern because in most cases you don't need more than one instance. At the very least, it is declared `final`.

Another example of pattern interaction is a Null Strategy, especially if a consumer is using multiple strategies one after another. For example, an ETL (Extract, Transform and Load) operation might mandate separate strategies for extracting data, transforming it in some way and then loading it into some sort of database. If you just want to read the data and store it without the data being transformed in any way, you might need a Null Strategy for the Transform part of the overall process.

A visitable Null Object can be useful as part of a hierarchy visited by the Visitor design pattern. For example, if every element of a mathematical expression is by definition a binary expression, a unary expression such as –X would have to be defined, in pseudocode, as `Subtract{Value{0},Value{X}}`. This may fail to be a workable solution because, were you to write a `PrinterVisitor` for printing such an expression, this visitor would print `0-X` instead of `-X`. Thus, you would instead define an expression as, perhaps, `Subtract{Null,Value{X}}` that would omit printing the `Null` value entirely, simply printing the remaining `-X` as intended. Some implementations of the Visitor design pattern could be taught to simply ignore the `Null` type completely.

The "classic" implementation of the State design pattern (see Chapter 21, "State") that performs state-driven state transitions may also optionally include a state which can potentially lack most or all behaviors. For example, a configurable traffic light system may consist of red, green, and amber states, with the amber state being optional. A client that does not need the amber state would supplant (perhaps inherit) the amber state such that, for example, a transition to that state will automatically result in a further transition to the next state. This naturally implies that the entire state machine is constructed in such a way as to make this sort of replacement possible.

Summary

The Null Object pattern raises an issue of API design: what kinds of assumptions can we make about the objects we depend upon? If we are taking a pointer (raw or smart), do we then have an obligation to check this pointer on every use?

If you feel no such obligation, then the only way the client can implement a Null Object is to construct a no-op implementation of the required interface and pass that instance where required. This only works well with functions, though: if the object's fields are also being used, for example, then you are in real trouble.

If you want to proactively support the idea of Null Objects being passed as arguments, you need to be explicit about it: either specify the parameter type as `std::optional`, give the parameter a default value that hints at a built-in Null Object (e.g., `= no_logging`), or just write documentation that explains what kind of value is expected at this location.

CHAPTER 20

Observer

The Observer pattern is a popular and necessary pattern, so it is surprising that, unlike other languages (e.g., C#), neither C++ nor the Standard Library comes with a ready-to-use implementation. Nonetheless, a safe, properly implemented Observer (if there can be such a thing) is a technically sophisticated construct, so in this chapter, we'll investigate it with all its gory details.

Property Observers

People get old. It's a fact of life. But when someone gets older by a year, we might want to congratulate them on their birthday. But how? Given a definition such as

```
struct Person
{
  int age;
  Person(int age) : age{age} {}
};
```

How do we know when a person's age changes? We don't. To see changes, we could try polling: reading a person's age every 100 milliseconds and comparing the new value with the previous. This approach will work but is tedious and does not scale. We need to be smarter about this.

© Dmitri Nesteruk 2022
D. Nesteruk, *Design Patterns in Modern C++20*,
https://doi.org/10.1007/978-1-4842-7295-4_20

We know that we want to be informed on every *write* to a person's age field. Well, the only way to catch this is to make a setter, that is:

```
struct Person
{
  int get_age() const { return age; }
  void set_age(const int value) { age = value; }
private:
  int age;
};
```

The setter set_age() is where we can notify whoever cares that age has, in fact, changed. But how?

Observer<T>

Well, one approach is to define some sort of base class that would need to be inherited by anyone interested in getting Person's changes:

```
struct PersonListener
{
  virtual void person_changed(Person& p,
    const string& property_name) = 0;
};
```

However, this approach is quite stifling because property changes can occur on types other than Person and we would not want to spawn additional classes for those too. Here's something a little more generic:

```
template<typename T> struct Observer
{
  virtual void field_changed(T& source,
    const string& field_name) = 0;
};
```

The two parameters in field_changed() are, hopefully, self-explanatory. The first is a reference to the object whose field actually changed, and the second is the name of the field. Yes, the name is passed as a string, which does hurt the refactorability of our code (what if the field name changes?).[1]

This implementation would allow us to observe changes to a Person class and, for example, write them to the command line:

```
struct ConsolePersonObserver : Observer<Person>
{
  void field_changed(Person& source, const string& field_name)
  override
  {
    if (field_name == "age")
    {
      cout << "Person's age has changed to "
           << source.get_age() << ".\n";
    }
  }
};
```

The flexibility we introduced into the scenario would allow us, for example, to observe property changes on multiple classes. For instance, if we add class Creature to the mix, you can now observe on both:

```
struct ConsolePersonObserver : Observer<Person>, Observer<Creature>
{
  void field_changed(Person& source, ...) { ... }
  void field_changed(Creature& source, ...) { ... }
};
```

---

[1] By contrast with C++, C# has explicitly solved this problem *twice* in successive releases. First, it introduced an attribute called [CallerMemberName] that inserted the name of calling function/property as the string value of a parameter. A second release simply introduced nameof(Foo) which would take the name of a symbol and turn it into a string.

Another alternative is to use `std::any` and do away with a generic implementation. Try it!

Observable<T>

Let's get back to the `Person` class. Since it is about to become an observable class, it has to take on new responsibilities, namely:

- Keeping a private list of all the observers interested in `Person`'s changes

- Letting the observers `subscribe()`/`unsubscribe()` to changes in `Person`

- Informing all observers when a change is actually made with `notify()`

All of this functionality can quite happily be moved to a separate base class so as to avoid replicating it for every potential observable:

```
template <typename T> struct Observable
{
  void notify(T& source, const string& name) { ... }
  void subscribe(Observer<T>* f) { observers.push_back(f); }
  void unsubscribe(Observer<T>* f) { ... }
private:
  vector<Observer<T>*> observers;
};
```

The `subscribe()` method just adds a new observer to the private list of observers. The list of observers isn't exposed to anyone – not even to the derived class. We don't want people arbitrarily manipulating this collection.

Next up, we need to implement notify(). The idea is simple – go through every observer and invoke its field_changed() one after another:

```
void notify(T& source, const string& name)
{
  for (auto obs : observers)
    obs->field_changed(source, name);
}
```

It's not enough to inherit from Observable<T>, though: our class also needs to do its part in calling notify() whenever a field is changed.

Consider the setter set_age(), for example. It now has three responsibilities:

- Check that the name has actually changed. If age is 20 and we are assigning 20 to it, there is no point performing any assignment or notification.

- Assign the field to the appropriate value.

- Call notify() with the right arguments.

Consequently, the new implementation of set_age() would look something like the following:

```
struct Person : Observable<Person>
{
  void set_age(const int age)
  {
    if (this->age == age) return;
    this->age = age;
    notify(*this, "age");
  }
private:
  int age;
};
```

Connecting Observers and Observables

We are now ready to start using the infrastructure we created in order to get notifications on Person's field changes (well, we could call them *properties*, really). Here's a reminder of what our observer looks like:

```cpp
struct ConsolePersonObserver : Observer<Person>
{
  void field_changed(Person& source,
    const string& field_name) override
  {
    cout << "Person's " << field_name << " has changed to "
        << source.get_age() << ".\n";
  }
};
```

And here is how we use it:

```cpp
Person p{ 20 };
ConsolePersonObserver cpo;
p.subscribe(&cpo);
p.set_age(21); // Person's age has changed to 21.
p.set_age(22); // Person's age has changed to 22.
```

So long as you don't concern yourself with issues around property dependencies and thread safety/reentrancy, you can stop here, take this implementation, and start using it. If you want to see discussions of more sophisticated approaches, read on.

Dependency Problems

People aged 16 or older (could be different in your country) can vote. So suppose we want to be notified of changes to a person's voting rights. First, let's assume that our Person type has the following getter:

```
bool get_can_vote() const { return age >= 16; }
```

Note that get_can_vote() has no backing field and no setter (we *could* introduce such a field, but it would be self-evidently redundant), yet we also feel obliged to notify() on it. But how? Well, we could try to find what *causes* can_vote to change... that's right, set_age() does! So if we want notifications on changes in voting status, these need to be done in set_age(). Get ready, you're in for a surprise!

```
void set_age(int value) const
{
  if (age == value) return;

  auto old_can_vote = can_vote(); // store old value
  age = value;
  notify(*this, "age");

  if (old_can_vote != can_vote()) // check value has changed
    notify(*this, "can_vote");
}
```

There's far too much happening inside this function. Not only do we check whether age has changed, we also check that can_vote has changed and notify on it too! You can probably guess this approach doesn't scale well, right? Imagine can_vote being dependent on *two* fields, say, age and citizenship – it means both of their setters have to handle can_vote notifications. And what if age also affects ten other properties this way? This is an unworkable solution that would lead to brittle code that's impossible to maintain, since relationships between variables need to be tracked manually.

In this scenario, can_vote is a *dependent property* of age. The challenge of dependent properties is essentially the challenge of tools such as Excel: given lots of dependencies between different cells, how do you know which cells to recalculate when one of them changes?

Property dependencies *can*, of course, be expressed some sort of map<string, vector<string>> what would keep a list of properties affected by a property (or, inversely, all the properties that affect a particular property). The sad thing is that this map would have to be defined by hand, and keeping it in sync with actual code is rather tricky.

Unsubscription and Thread Safety

One thing that I've neglected to discuss is how an observer might unsubscribe() from an observable. Generally, you want to remove yourself from the list of observers, which, in a single-threaded scenario, is as simple as

```
void unsubscribe(Observer<T>* observer)
{
  observers.erase(
    remove(observers.begin(), observers.end(), observer),
    observers.end());
};
```

While the use of the erase-remove idiom is technically correct, it is only correct in a single-threaded scenario. std::vector is not thread-safe, so calling, say, subscribe() and unsubscribe() at the same time could lead to unintended consequences, since both methods modify the vector.

This is easily cured by simply putting a lock on all of observable's operations:

```cpp
template <typename T> struct Observable
{
  void notify(T& source, const string& name)
  {
    scoped_lock<mutex> lock{ mtx };
    ...
  }
  void subscribe(Observer<T>* f)
  {
    scoped_lock<mutex> lock{ mtx };
    ...
  }
  void unsubscribe(Observer<T>* o)
  {
    scoped_lock<mutex> lock{ mtx };
    ...
  }
private:
  vector<Observer<T>*> observers;
  mutex mtx;
};
```

Another, very viable, alternative is to use something like a concurrent_ vector from PPL/TPL.[2] Naturally you lose ordering guarantees (in other words, adding two objects one after another doesn't guarantee they are notified in order), but it certainly saves you from having to manage locks yourself.

---

[2] The Microsoft Parallel Patterns Library and the Intel Task Parallel Library (TPL) have similar thread-safe container classes.

Reentrancy

The last implementation provides some thread safety through locking any of the three key methods whenever someone needs it. But now let's imagine the following scenario: you have a TrafficAdministration component that keeps monitoring a person until they're old enough to drive. When they're 17, the component unsubscribes:

```
struct TrafficAdministration : Observer<Person>
{
  void TrafficAdministration::field_changed(
    Person& source, const string& field_name) override
  {
    if (field_name == "age")
    {
      if (source.get_age() < 17)
        cout << "Whoa there, you are not old enough to
        drive!\n";
      else
      {
        // oh, ok, they are old enough, let's not monitor them
           anymore
        cout << "We no longer care!\n";
        source.unsubscribe(this);
      }
    }
  }
};
```

When age turns to 17, the overall chain of calls will be

```
notify() --> field_changed() --> unsubscribe()
```

This is a problem because, in `unsubscribe()`, we end up trying to take a lock that's already taken. This is a *reentrancy* problem. There are different ways to handle this:

- One way is to simply prohibit such situations. After all, at least in this particular case, it's very obvious that reentrancy is taking place here.

- Another way is to bail out on the idea of removing elements from the collection. Instead, we could go for something like

```
void unsubscribe(Observer<T>* o)
{
  auto it = find(observers.begin(), observers.end(), o);
  if (it != observers.end())
    *it = nullptr;
}
```

And, subsequently, when you `notify()`, you just need an extra check:

```
void notify(T& source, const string& name)
{
for (auto obs : observers)
  if (obs)
    obs->field_changed(source, name);
}
```

Of course, this only solves possible contention between `notify()` and `subscribe()`. If you were to, for example, `subscribe()` and `unsubscribe()` at the same time, this is still concurrent modification of a collection – and it can still fail. So, at the very least, you might want to keep a lock there.

Yet another possibility is to just make a copy of the entire collection in notify(). You *do* need the lock still; you just don't apply it to notifications. Here's what I mean:

```
void notify(T& source, const string& name)
{
  vector<Observer<T>*> observers_copy;
  {
    lock_guard<mutex_t> lock{ mtx };
    observers_copy = observers;
  }
  for (auto obs : observers_copy)
    if (obs)
      obs->field_changed(source, name);
}
```

In this implementation, we do take a lock, but, by the time we call field_changed, the lock has been released, since it's only created in the artificial scope used to copy the vector. I wouldn't worry about efficiency here, since a vector of pointers doesn't take up that much memory.

Finally, it's always possible to replace a mutex by a recursive_mutex. Generally speaking, recursive mutexes are hated by most developers (plenty of proof can be found on StackOverflow), not just due to performance implications but more due to the fact that in the majority of cases (just like Observer example), you can get away with using ordinary, non-recursive variants if you design your code a bit better.

There are some interesting practical concerns that we haven't really discussed here. They include the following:

- What happens if the same observer is added twice?

- If I allow duplicate observers, does ubsubscribe() remove every single instance?

- How is the behavior affected if we use a different container? For example, we decide to prevent duplicates by using an `std::set` or `boost::unordered_set`; what does this imply for ordinary operations?

- What if I want observers that are ranked by priority?

These and other practical concerns are all manageable once your foundations are solid. We won't spend further time discussing them here.

Observer with Boost.Signals2

There are many prepackaged implementation of the Observer pattern, and probably the most well known is the Boost.Signals2 library.[3] Essentially, this library provides a type called `signal` that represents a *signal* in C++ terminology (called *event* elsewhere). This signal can be subscribed to by providing a function or lambda. It can also be unsubscribed to and, when you want to notify on this, it can be fired.

Using Boost.Signals2, we can define `Observable<T>`:

```
template <typename T>
struct Observable
{
  signal<void(T&, const string&)> property_changed;
};
```

---

[3] See `www.boost.org/doc/libs/1_76_0/doc/html/signals2.html` for more info.

And its invocation looks as follows:

```
struct Person : Observable<Person>
{
  ...
  void set_age(const int age)
  {
    if (this->age == age) return;
    this->age = age;
    property_changed(*this, "age");
  }
};
```

The actual use of the API would directly use the signal unless, of course, you decided to add member functions to make it easier:

```
Person p{123};
auto conn = p.property_changed.connect([](Person&, const
string& prop_name)
{
  cout << prop_name << " has been changed" << endl;
});
p.set_age(20); // age has been changed

// later, optionally
conn.disconnect();
```

The result of a connect() call is a connection object that can also be used to unsubscribe when you no longer need notifications from the signal.

Views

There's a big, huge, glaring problem with property observers: the approach is intrusive and clearly goes against the idea of separation of concerns. Change notification is a separate concern, so adding it right into your domain objects might not be the best idea – especially considering that it is only one of a number of concerns (others include validation, automatic data type conversions, etc.) that may become evident at a later stage once the domain is already well defined.

So, imagine you decide to change your mind and move from the use of Observable<T> to the use of some completely different construct. If you had scattered Observable throughout your domain objects, you'd have to meticulously go through each one, modifying each property to use the new paradigm, not to mention the fact that you'd have to modify those classes as well to stop using the old interfaces and start using the new ones. This is tedious and error-prone and precisely the kind of thing we're trying to avoid.

So, if you want change notifications handled outside of the objects that change, where would you add them? It shouldn't be hard – after all, we've seen patterns such as Decorator that are designed for this exact purpose.

One approach is to put another object in front of your domain object that would handle change notifications and other things besides. This is what we would typically called a *view* – it is this thing that would be bound to UI, for example.

To use views, you would keep your objects simple, using ordinary properties (or even public fields!) without embellishing them with any extra behaviors:

```
struct Person
{
  string name;
};
```

In fact, it's worth keeping the data objects as simple as possible; this is what's known as a *data class* in languages such as Kotlin. Now what you do is build a view on top of the object. The view can incorporate other concerns, including property observers:

```
struct PersonView : Observable<Person>
{
  explicit PersonView(const Person& person)
    : person(person) {}

  string& get_name()
  {
    return person.name;
  }
  void set_name(const string& value)
  {
    if (value != person.name) return;
    person.name = value;
    property_changed(person, "name");
  }
protected:
  Person& person;
};
```

This view we've created is, of course, a Decorator. It wraps the underlying object with getters/setters that perform the notifications. If you need even more complexity, this is the place to add it.

Now, with the view constructed, it can be plugged into the rest of the application. For example, if your app has a user interface with an editable text field, that field could interact with name getter and setter in the view.

Summary

Let's recap the main design decisions when implementing Observer:

- Decide what information you want your observable to communicate. For example, if you are handling field/property changes, you can include the name of the property. You can also specify old/new values, but passing the type could be problematic.

- Do you want your observers to be entire classes, or are you OK with just having a list of virtual functions?

- How do you want to handle observers unsubscribing?

  - If you don't plan to support unsubscription, congratulations, you'll save a lot of effort implementing the Observer since there are no removal issues in reentrancy scenarios.

  - If you plan to support an explicit unsubscribe() function, maybe you don't want to erase-remove right in the function, but instead mark your elements for removal and remove them later?

  - If you don't like the idea of dispatching on a (possibly null) raw pointer, consider using a weak_ptr instead.

- Will the functions of an Observer<T> be invoked from several different threads? If they are, you need to protect your subscription list:

  - You can put a scoped_lock on all relevant functions.

  - Or you can use a thread-safe collection such as the TBB/PPL concurrent_vector. You lose ordering guarantees but get thread safety, not such a bad trade-off.

- Are multiple subscriptions from the same source allowed? If they are, you cannot use an std::set.

Without a doubt, some of the code presented in this chapter is an example of overthinking and overengineering a problem way beyond what most people would want to achieve.

There is, sadly, no ideal implementation of Observer that ticks all the boxes. Whichever implementation you go for, some compromises are expected.

CHAPTER 21

State

I must confess: my behavior is governed by my state. If I didn't get enough sleep, I'm going to be a bit tired. If I had a drink, I wouldn't get behind the wheel. All of these are *states* and they govern my behavior: how I feel, what I can and cannot do.

I can, of course, transition from one state to another. I can go get a coffee, and this will take me from sleepy to alert (I hope!). So we can think of coffee as a *trigger* that causes a transition of yours truly from sleepy to just about awake. Here, let me clumsily illustrate it for you:[1]

```
          coffee
sleepy --------> alert
```

So, the State design pattern is a very simple idea: state controls behavior, state can be changed, the only thing which the jury is out on is *who* triggers the state change.

There are, fundamentally, two ways:

- States are actual classes with behaviors, and these behaviors switch the actual state from one to another.

- States and transitions are just enumerations. We have a special component called a *state machine* that performs the actual transitions.

---

[1] I don't actually drink coffee. This is just of the many white lies I have woven into this book :)

© Dmitri Nesteruk 2022
D. Nesteruk, *Design Patterns in Modern C++20*,
https://doi.org/10.1007/978-1-4842-7295-4_21

Both of these approaches are viable, but it's really the second approach that is the most common. We'll take a look at both of them, but I must admit I'll glance over the first one, since this isn't how people typically do things.

State-Driven State Transitions

We'll begin with the most trivial example out there: a light switch. It can only be in the *on* and *off* states. We're going to build a model where any state is capable of switching to some other state: while this reflects the "classic" implementation of the State design pattern (as per GoF book), it's not something I'd recommend.

First, let's model the light switch. All it has is a pointer to the current state and some means of switching from one state to another:

```
class LightSwitch
{
  State *state{nullptr};
public:
  LightSwitch()
  {
    state = new OffState();
  }
  void set_state(State* state)
  {
    this->state = state;
  }
};
```

This all looks perfectly reasonable. We can now define the State which, in this particular case, is going to be an actual class.

```cpp
struct State
{
  virtual void on(LightSwitch *ls)
  {
    cout << "Light is already on\n";
  }
  virtual void off(LightSwitch *ls)
  {
    cout << "Light is already off\n";
  }
};
```

This implementation is far from intuitive, so much so that we need to discuss it slowly and carefully, because from the outset, nothing about the State class makes sense.

First of all, State is not abstract! You'd think that a state you have no way (or reason!) of reaching would be abstract. But it's not.

Second, State allows the switching from one state to another. This… to a reasonable person, it makes no sense. Imagine the light switch: it's the switch that changes states. The state itself isn't expected to change *itself*, and yet it appears this is exactly what it does.

Third, perhaps most bewildering, the default behavior of State::on/off claims that we are *already* in this state! This will come together, somewhat, as we implement the rest of the example.

We now implement the On and Off states:

```
struct OnState : State
{
  OnState() { cout << "Light turned on\n"; }
  void off(LightSwitch* ls) override;
};

struct OffState : State
{
  OffState() { cout << "Light turned off\n"; }
  void on(LightSwitch* ls) override;
};
```

The implementations of OnState::off and OffState::on allow the state itself to switch itself to another state! Here's what it looks like:

```
void OnState::off(LightSwitch* ls)
{
  cout << "Switching light off...\n";
  ls->set_state(new OffState());
  delete this;
} // same for OffState::on
```

So this is where the switching happens. This implementation contains the bizarre invocation of delete this, something you don't often see in real-world C++. delete this makes a very dangerous assumption of where the state is initially allocated. The example could be rewritten with, say, smart pointers, but using ordinary pointers and heap allocation highlights clearly that the state is being actively destroyed here. If the state had a destructor, it would trigger and you would perform additional cleanup here.

Of course, we do want the switch itself to switch states too, which looks like this:

```
class LightSwitch
{
  ...
  void on() { state->on(this); }
  void off() { state->off(this); }
};
```

So, putting it all together, we can run the following scenario:

```
LightSwitch ls; // Light turned off
ls.on();        // Switching light on...
                // Light turned on
ls.off();       // Switching light off...
                // Light turned off
ls.off();       // Light is already off
```

I must admit: I don't like this approach, because it is not intuitive. Sure, the state can be informed (Observer pattern) that we're moving into it. But the idea of state switching itself to another state – which is the "classic" implementation of the State pattern as per the GoF book – doesn't seem particularly palatable.

If we were to clumsily illustrate a transition from OffState to OnState, it needs to be illustrated as

```
         LightSwitch::on() -> OffState::on()
OffState -----------------------------------> OnState
```

On the other hand, the transition from OnState to OnState uses the base State class, the one that tells you that you are already in that state:

```
         LightSwitch::on() -> State::on()
OnState -------------------------------> OnState
```

The example presented here may seem particularly artificial, so we are now going to look at another handmade set-up, one where the states and transitions are reduced to enumeration members.

Handmade State Machine

Let us try to define a state machine for a typical phone conversation. First of all, we'll describe the states of a phone:

```
enum class State
{
  off_hook,
  connecting,
  connected,
  on_hold,
  on_hook
};
```

We can now also define transitions between states, also as an enum class:

```
enum class Trigger
{
  call_dialed,
  hung_up,
  call_connected,
  placed_on_hold,
  taken_off_hold,
  left_message,
  stop_using_phone
};
```

Now, the exact *rules* of this state machine, that is, what transitions are possible, need to be stored somewhere.

```
map<State, vector<pair<Trigger, State>>> rules;
```

This is a little clumsy, but essentially the key of the map is the State we're moving *from,* and the value is a set of Trigger-State pairs representing possible triggers while in this state and the state you move into when you use the trigger.

Let's initialize this data structure:

```
rules[State::off_hook] = {
  {Trigger::call_dialed, State::connecting},
  {Trigger::stop_using_phone, State::on_hook}
};

rules[State::connecting] = {
  {Trigger::hung_up, State::off_hook},
  {Trigger::call_connected, State::connected}
};
// more rules here
```

We also need a starting state, and we can also add an exit (terminal) state if we want the state machine to stop executing once that state is reached:

```
State currentState{ State::off_hook },
      exitState{ State::on_hook };
```

Having made this, we don't necessarily have to build a separate component for actually running (we use the term *orchestrating*) a state machine. For example, if we wanted to build an interactive model of the telephone, we could do it thus:

```
while (true)
{
  cout << "The phone is currently " << currentState << endl;
select_trigger:
  cout << "Select a trigger:" << "\n";

  int i = 0;
  for (auto item : rules[currentState])
  {
    cout << i++ << ". " << item.first << "\n";
  }

  int input;
  cin >> input;
  if (input < 0 || (input+1) > rules[currentState].size())
  {
    cout << "Incorrect option. Please try again." << "\n";
    goto select_trigger;
  }

  currentState = rules[currentState][input].second;
  if (currentState == exitState) break;
}
```

First of all, yes, I do use goto; this is a good illustration of where it's appropriate. As for the algorithm itself, we let the user select one of the available triggers on the current state (operator << has been implemented for both State and Trigger behind the scenes), and, provided the trigger is valid, we transition to it by using that rules map that we created earlier.

Finally, if the state we've reached is the exit state, we jump out of the loop. Here's a sample interaction with the program:

```
The phone is currently off the hook
Select a trigger:
0. call dialed
1. putting phone on hook
0
The phone is currently connecting
Select a trigger:
0. hung up
1. call connected
1
The phone is currently connected
Select a trigger:
0. left message
1. hung up
2. placed on hold
2
The phone is currently on hold
Select a trigger:
0. taken off hold
1. hung up
1
The phone is currently off the hook
Select a trigger:
0. call dialed
1. putting phone on hook
1
We are done using the phone
```

This hand-rolled state machine's main benefit is that it is very easy to understand: states and transitions are ordinary enumerations, the set of transitions is defined in a simple `std::map`, and the start and end states are simple variables.

Switch-Based State Machine

In our exploration of state machines, we have progressed from the needlessly complicated classic example where states are represented by classes to a handcrafted example where states are represented as enumeration members, and now we shall experience one final step of degradation, as we stop using dedicated data types for transitions.

But our simplifications won't end there: instead of jumping from one method call to another, we'll confine ourselves to an infinitely repeating `switch` statement where state will be examined and transitions will happen by virtue of the state changing.

The scenario I want you to consider is a combination lock. The lock has a four-digit code (e.g., `1234`) that you enter one digit at a time. As you enter the code, if you make a mistake, you get the `"FAILED"` output, but if you enter all digits correctly, you get `"UNLOCKED"` instead and you exit the state machine.

We shall still encode the states using an enumeration:

```
enum class State
{
  locked,
  failed,
  unlocked
};
```

The entire scenario that we want to run can fit into a single listing:

```cpp
const string code{"1274"};
auto state{State::locked};
string entry;

while (true)
{
  switch (state)
  {
  case State::locked:
    {
      entry += (char)getchar();
      getchar(); // consume return

      if (entry == code)
      {
        state = State::unlocked;
        break;
      }

      if (!code.starts_with(entry))
      {
        state = State::failed;
      }
      break;
    }
  case State::failed:
    cout << "FAILED\n";
    return;
```

```
    case State::unlocked:
      cout << "UNLOCKED\n";
      return;
    }
}
```

Here's a sample interaction if you use the correct code:

```
1
2
3
4
UNLOCKED
```

Here's an interaction if you make an error during the code entry process:

```
1
2
7
FAILED
```

As you can see, this is still very much a state machine, albeit one that lacks any structure. You couldn't examine it from the top level and be able to tell what all the possible states and transitions are. It is not clear, unless you really examine the code, how the transitions happen – and we're lucky there are no goto statements here to make jumps between the cases!

This Switch-Based State Machine approach is viable for scenarios with very small numbers of states and transitions. It loses out on structure, readability, and maintainability but can work as a quick patch if you do need a state machine quickly and are too lazy to make a list of all the transition rules as a separate data structure.

Overall, this approach does not scale and is difficult to manage, so I would not recommend it in production code. The only exception would be if such a machine was made using code generation on the basis of some external model.

State Machines with Boost.MSM

In the real world, state machines are more complicated. Sometimes, you want some action to occur when a state is reached. At other times, you want transitions to be *conditional*, that is, you want a transition to occur only if some condition predicate is satisfied.

When using Boost.MSM (Meta State Machine), a state machine library that's part of Boost, your state machine is a class that inherits from state_ machine_def via CRTP:

```
struct PhoneStateMachine : state_machine_def<PhoneStateMachine>
{
  bool angry{ false };
```

I've added a bool indicating whether the caller is angry (because of being put on hold); we'll use it a little bit later. Now, each state can also reside in the state machine and is expected to inherit from the state class:

```
struct OffHook : state<> {};
struct Connecting : state<>
{
  template <class Event, class FSM>
  void on_entry(Event const& evt, FSM&)
  {
    cout << "We are connecting..." << endl;
  }
  // also on_exit
};
// other states omitted
```

As you can see, the state can also define behaviors that happen when you enter or exit a particular state.

You can also define behaviors to be executed on a transition (rather than when you've reached a state). Transitions are also classes, but they don't need to inherit from anything; instead, they need to provide operator() with a particular signature:

```
struct PhoneBeingDestroyed
{
  template <class EVT, class FSM, class SourceState, class
  TargetState>
  void operator()(EVT const&, FSM&, SourceState&, TargetState&)
  {
    cout << "Phone breaks into a million pieces" << endl;
  }
};
```

As you may have guessed, the arguments give you references to the state machine and the states you're going from and to.

Lastly, we have *guard conditions*: these dictate whether or not we can actually use a transition in the first place. Now, our Boolean variable angry is not in the form usable by MSM, so we need to wrap it:

```
struct CanDestroyPhone
{
  template <class EVT, class FSM, class SourceState, class
  TargetState>
  bool operator()(EVT const&, FSM& fsm, SourceState&,
  TargetState&)
  {
    return fsm.angry;
  }
};
```

This defines a guard condition called CanDestroyPhone, which we can later use when we define the state machine.

For defining state machine rules, Boost.MSM uses MPL (MetaProgramming Library). Specifically, the transition table is defined as an mpl::vector with each row containing, in turn,

- The source state

- The transition

- The target state

- An optional action to execute

- An optional guard condition

So with all of that, we can define some phone-calling rules as follows:

```
struct transition_table : mpl::vector <
  Row<OffHook, CallDialed, Connecting>,
  Row<Connecting, CallConnected, Connected>,
  Row<Connected, PlacedOnHold, OnHold>,
  Row<OnHold, PhoneThrownIntoWall, PhoneDestroyed,
      PhoneBeingDestroyed, CanDestroyPhone>
> {};
```

The last row of our transition_table is the most interesting: it specifies that we can only attempt to destroy phone subject to the CanDestroyPhone guard condition, and when the phone is actually being destroyed, the PhoneBeingDestroyed action should be executed.

Unlike states, transitions such as CallDialed are classes that can be defined *outside* the state machine class. They don't have to inherit from any base class and can easily be empty, but they do have to be types.

Now, there are a couple more things we can add. First, we add the starting condition, and since we're using Boost.MSM, the starting condition is a typedef, not a variable:

```
typedef OffHook initial_state;
```

Finally, we can define an action to occur if there are no possible transitions. It could happen! For example, after you smash the phone, you cannot use it anymore, right?

```
template <class FSM, class Event>
void no_transition(Event const& e, FSM&, int state)
{
  cout << "No transition from state " << state_names[state]
    << " on event " << typeid(e).name() << endl;
}
```

Boost MSM divides the state machine into the front end (that's what we just wrote) and the back end (the part that runs it). Using the back-end API, we can construct the state machine from our state machine definition:

```
msm::back::state_machine<PhoneStateMachine> phone;
```

Now, assuming the existence of the info() function which just prints the state we're in, we can try orchestrating the following scenario:

```
info(); // The phone is currently off hook
phone.process_event(CallDialed{}); // We are connecting...
info(); // The phone is currently connecting
phone.process_event(CallConnected{});
info(); // The phone is currently connected
phone.process_event(PlacedOnHold{});
info(); // The phone is currently on hold
```

```
phone.process_event(PhoneThrownIntoWall{});
// Phone breaks into a million pieces

info(); // The phone is currently destroyed

phone.process_event(CallDialed{});
// No transition from state destroyed on event struct
   CallDialed
```

So this is how you define a more sophisticated, industry-strength state machine.

Summary

First of all, it's worth highlighting that Boost.MSM is one of two alternative state machine implementations in Boost, the other being Boost.Statechart. I'm pretty sure there are plenty of other state machine implementations out there.

Secondly, there's a lot more to state machines than that. For example, many libraries support the idea of *hierarchical* state machines: for example, a state of Sick can *contain* many different substates such as Flu or Chickenpox. If you are in state Flu, you are also assumed to be in the state Sick.

Finally, it's worth highlighting again how far modern state machines are from the State design pattern in its original form. The existence of duplicate APIs (e.g., LightSwitch::on/off vs. State::on/off) as well as the presence of self-deletion are definite code smells. Don't get me wrong – the approach works, but it's unintuitive and cumbersome.

CHAPTER 22

Strategy

You'll be surprised to know that you have probably used the Strategy pattern in your everyday interactions with the Standard Library. After all, any time you specify a particular sorting algorithm, for example, you are specifying a sorting *strategy*, that is, providing a partial definition of the overall algorithm:

```cpp
vector<int> values{3,1,5,2,4};
sort(values.begin(), values.end(), less<>{});
for (int x : values)
  cout << x << ' '; // 1 2 3 4 5
```

In the preceding, the function `less` is a sorting strategy for the overall sorting algorithm. `less` is simply a wrapper template function for the `<` operator, so the sorting operation gets us elements from the smallest to the largest.

In functional programming parlance, `sort()` is a *higher-order function*, that is, a function that takes other functions. C++ provides two ways of making it happen:

- A function takes a function as a template parameter. This is unfriendly to the client because code completion hints will offer no information about what the signature of the function argument should be.

- A function takes a function as a proper function pointer, std::function, or something similar. This is a lot more friendly because you can tell what form the function parameter should take.

As for the way the functional parameter is actually constructed, well, in the case of algorithms such as sort(), the strategy can be provided either as a reference to some callable construct (e.g., a functor) or you can provide it in place by using a lambda:

```
vector<int> values{3,1,5,2,4};
sort(values.begin(), values.end(),
    [=](int a, int b) { return a > b; });
for (int x : values)
  cout << x << ' '; // 5 4 3 2 1
```

While the strategy used in a sort() is perishable (it only lives for the duration of the call), nothing prevents you from saving the strategy in a variable and then reusing it whenever necessary. There are many advantages to defining strategies as classes, including

- A class-based strategy can be stateful.

- A strategy can be composed of several methods, all describing constituent parts of a strategy.

- Strategies can inherit other strategies, which allows for easy reuse.

- Strategy dependencies can be described using interfaces rather than function signatures.

- A chosen default strategy can be configured in an IoC container.

In other words, defining strategies as classes can be useful, particularly when strategies are complicated, configurable, or composed of multiple parts.

In C++ parlance, another word for strategy is *policy*.

Dynamic Strategy

Suppose you decide to take an array or vector of several strings and output them as a list,

- just

- like

- this

If you think about the different output formats, you probably know that you need to take each element and output it with some additional markup. But in the case of languages such as HTML or LaTeX, the list will also need the start and end tags or markers.

We can formulate a strategy for rendering a list:

- Render the opening tag/element.

- For each of the list items, render that item.

- Render the closing tag/element.

Different strategies can be formulated for different output formats, and these strategies can be then fed into a general, non-changing algorithm to generate the text.

This is yet another pattern that exists in dynamic (runtime-replaceable) and static (template-composed, fixed) incarnations. Let's take a look at both of them.

Our goal is to print a simple list of text items in the following format:

```
enum class OutputFormat
{
  markdown,
  html
};
```

The skeleton of our strategy will be defined in the following base class:

```
struct ListStrategy
{
  virtual void start(ostringstream& oss) {};
  virtual void add_list_item(ostringstream& oss,
    const string& item) {};
  virtual void end(ostringstream& oss) {};
};
```

A design decision has been made to make the base class nonabstract; this way, it's effectively a kind of Null Object (should you ever need one). The intent is that inheritors can override only the necessary methods while leaving others with their no-op implementations.

Now let us jump to our text processing component. This component would have a list-specific member function called, say, append_list().

```
struct TextProcessor
{
  void append_list(const vector<string> items)
  {
    list_strategy->start(oss);
    for (auto& item : items)
      list_strategy->add_list_item(oss, item);
```

```
    list_strategy->end(oss);
  }
private:
  ostringstream oss;
  unique_ptr<ListStrategy> list_strategy;
};
```

We've got a buffer called `oss` where all the output goes, the strategy that we're using for rendering lists, and of course `append_list()` which specifies the set of steps that need to be taken to actually render a list with a given strategy.

Now, pay attention here. Composition, as used here, is one of two possible options that can be taken to allow concrete implementations of a skeleton algorithm. Instead, we could add functions such as `add_list_item()` as virtual members to be overridden by derived classes: that's what the Template Method pattern does.

Anyways, back to our discussion. We can now go ahead and implement different strategies for lists, such as a `HtmlListStrategy`:

```
struct HtmlListStrategy : ListStrategy
{
  void start(ostringstream& oss) override
  {
    oss << "<ul>\n";
  }
  void end(ostringstream& oss) override
  {
    oss << "</ul>\n";
  }
  void add_list_item(ostringstream& oss, const string& item)
  override
  {
```

```
    oss << "  <li>" << item << "</li>\n";
  }
};
```

By implementing the overrides, we fill in the gaps that specify how to process lists. We would implement a MarkdownListStrategy in a similar fashion, but because Markdown does not need opening/closing tags, we would only override the add_list_item() function:

```
struct MarkdownListStrategy : ListStrategy
{
  void add_list_item(ostringstream& oss,
                     const string& item) override
  {
    oss << " * " << item;
  }
};
```

We can now start using the TextProcessor, feeding it different strategies and getting different results, for example:

```
TextProcessor tp{OutputFormat::markdown};
tp.append_list({"foo", "bar", "baz"});
cout << tp.str() << endl;
// * foo
// * bar
// * baz
```

We can make provisions for strategies to be switchable at runtime – this is precisely why we call this implementation a *dynamic* strategy. This is done in the set_output_format() function, whose implementation is trivial:

```
void set_output_format(const OutputFormat format)
{
  switch(format)
  {
  case OutputFormat::markdown:
    list_strategy = make_unique<MarkdownListStrategy>();
    break;
  case OutputFormat::html:
    list_strategy = make_unique<HtmlListStrategy>();
    break;
  }
}
```

Now, switching from one strategy to another is simple, and you get to see the results straightaway:

```
tp.clear(); // clears the text processor's buffer
tp.set_output_format(OutputFormat::Html);
tp.append_list({"foo", "bar", "baz"});
cout << tp.str() << endl;
// <ul>
//   <li>foo</li>
//   <li>bar</li>
//   <li>baz</li>
// </ul>
```

Static Strategy

Thanks to the magic of templates, you can bake any strategy right into the type. Only minimal changes are necessary to the TextStrategy class:

```
template <typename LS>
struct TextProcessor
{
  void append_list(const vector<string> items)
  {
    list_strategy.start(oss);
    for (auto& item : items)
      list_strategy.add_list_item(oss, item);
    list_strategy.end(oss);
  }
  // other functions unchanged
private:
  ostringstream oss;
  LS list_strategy; // strategy instantiated here
};
```

All that's changed is that we added the LS template argument, made a member strategy with this type, and started using it instead of the pointer we had previously. The results of append_list() are identical.

```
// markdown
TextProcessor<MarkdownListStrategy> tpm;
tpm.append_list({"foo", "bar", "baz"});
cout << tpm.str() << endl;

// html
TextProcessor<HtmlListStrategy> tph;
tph.append_list({"foo", "bar", "baz"});
cout << tph.str() << endl;
```

The output from the preceding example is the same as for the dynamic strategy. Note that we've had to make two instances of `TextProcessor`, each with a distinct list-handling strategy.

Summary

The Strategy design pattern allows you to define a skeleton of an algorithm and then use composition to supply the missing implementation details. This approach exists in different incarnations:

- *Functional strategy* is when a strategy is passed as a functor or lambda that you (typically) do not intend to hold on to.

- *Dynamic strategy* keeps a pointer/reference to the strategy being used. Want to change to a different strategy? Just change the reference. Easy!

- *Static strategy* requires that you choose the strategy at compile time and stick with it – there is no scope for changing your mind later on.

Should one use dynamic or static strategies? Well, dynamic ones allow reconfiguration of the objects after they have been constructed. Imagine a UI setting which controls the form of the textual output: what would you rather have, a switchable `TextProcessor` or two variables of type `TextProcessor<MarkdownStrategy>` and `TextProcessor<HtmlStrategy>`? It's really up to you.

On a final note, you can constrain the set of strategies a type takes: instead of allowing a general `ListStrategy` argument, one can take an `std::variant` that lists the only permitted types that can be passed in.

CHAPTER 23

Template Method

The Strategy and Template Method design patterns are very similar, so much so that, just like with Factories, I would be very tempted to merge those patterns into a single Skeleton Method design pattern. I will resist the urge.

The difference between Strategy and Template Method is that Strategy uses composition (whether static or dynamic), whereas Template Method uses inheritance. But the core principle of defining the skeleton of an algorithm in one place and its implementation details in other places remain, once again observing the Open-Closed Principle.

Game Simulation

Most board games are very similar: the game starts (some sort of set-up takes place), players take turns until a winner is decided, and then the winner can be announced. It doesn't matter what the game is – chess, checkers, or something else – we can define the algorithm as follows:

```cpp
class Game
{
  void run()
  {
    start();
    while (!have_winner())
```

© Dmitri Nesteruk 2022
D. Nesteruk, *Design Patterns in Modern C++20*,
https://doi.org/10.1007/978-1-4842-7295-4_23

```
    take_turn();
  cout << "Player " << get_winner() << " wins.\n";
}
```

As you can see, the run() method, which runs the game, simply calls a set of other methods. These are pure virtual methods and also have protected visibility, so they don't get accidentally invoked on their own:

```
protected:
  virtual void start() = 0;
  virtual bool have_winner() = 0;
  virtual void take_turn() = 0;
  virtual int get_winner() = 0;
```

To be fair, some of these methods, especially void-returning ones, do not necessarily have to be pure virtual. For example, if some games have no explicit start() procedure, having start() as pure virtual violates ISP, since members which do not need it would still have to implement it. In Chapter 22, "Strategy," we deliberately made a strategy with virtual no-op methods, but with Template Method, the case is not so clear-cut.

Now, in addition to these members, we can have certain public members that are relevant to all games – the number of players and the index of the current player:

```
class Game
{
public:
  explicit Game(int number_of_players)
    : number_of_players{number_of_players} {}
protected:
  int current_player{ 0 };
  int number_of_players;
}; // other members omitted
```

From here on out, the Game class can be extended to implement a game of chess:

```
class Chess : public Game
{
public:
  explicit Chess() : Game{ 2 } {}
protected:
  void start() override {}
  bool have_winner() override { return turns == max_turns; }
  void take_turn() override
  {
    turns++;
    current_player = (current_player + 1) % number_of_players;
  }
  int get_winner() override { return current_player;}
private:
  int turns{ 0 }, max_turns{ 10 };
};
```

A game of chess involves two players, so that's fed into the constructor. We then proceed to override all the necessary functions, implementing some very simple simulation logic for ending the game after ten turns. Here is the output:

```
Starting a game of chess with 2 players
Turn 0 taken by player 0
Turn 1 taken by player 1
...
Turn 8 taken by player 0
Turn 9 taken by player 1
Player 0 wins.
```

And that's pretty much all there is to it!

Functional Template Method

While the canonical template method leverages inheritance, Modern C++ also allows for a functional variation. In this case, the lines are greatly blurred between the Strategy and Template Method design patterns because, in both, we are essentially talking about higher-order functions.

The functional approach to Template Method is to simply define a stand-alone function run_game() that takes the templated parts as parameters. As always, when defining a higher-order function, we have two options:

- Strongly typing the accepted functions as function pointers, std::functions, or similar constructs.

- Using templates to loosely define the parameters. This lets us pass in diverse structures, from functors to lambdas, as parameters.

Our functional definition will still feature a structure that collects some information about a game:

```
struct GameState
{
  int current_player, winning_player;
  int number_of_players;
};
```

We now define the template method as before, the only difference being that it's not part of any class, and, as a result, instead of using members that are meant to be overridden, all those members get turned into template parameters:

```
template<typename FnStartAction,
  typename FnTakeTurnAction,
  typename FnHaveWinnerAction>
```

```
void run_game(GameState initial_state,
              FnStartAction start_action,
              FnTakeTurnAction take_turn_action,
              FnHaveWinnerAction have_winner_action)
{
  GameState state = initial_state;
  start_action(state);
  while (!have_winner_action(state))
  {
    take_turn_action(state);
  }
  cout << "Player " << state.winning_player << " wins.\n";
}
```

Our run_game() takes the initial state and a bunch of functions or function-like objects. These can be defined anywhere – you can use heavy constructs such as functors, but it's easy to just define a couple of lambda functions:

```
int turn{0}, max_turns{10};
GameState state{0, -1, 2};

auto start = [](GameState& s)
{
  cout << "Starting a game of chess with " <<
    s.number_of_players << " players\n";
};

auto take_turn = [&](GameState& s)
{
  cout << "Turn " << turn++ << " taken by player"
    << s.current_player << "\n";
```

```
  s.current_player = (s.current_player + 1) % s.number_of_
  players;
  s.winning_player = s.current_player;
};

auto have_winner = [&](GameState& s)
{
  return turn == max_turns;
};
```

Note that we also define some additional state (specific to our simulation) that our lambda functions use. With all of this assembled, we can call our template method:

```
run_game(state, start, take_turn, have_winner);
```

The output of this program is exactly as before.

Summary

Unlike the Strategy, which uses composition and thus branches into static and dynamic variations, Template Method uses inheritance, and, as a consequence, it can only be static, since there is no way to fiddle the inheritance characteristics of an object once it's been constructed.

The only design decision in a Template Method is whether you want the methods used by the Template Method to be pure virtual or actually have a body, even if that body is empty. If you foresee some methods being unnecessary for some inheritors, go ahead and make them no-op ones.

A functional variation of Template Method blurs the lines between Strategy and Template Method, since it doesn't leverage OOP. It is not as user-friendly as the OOP variety since it doesn't group related functions together and doesn't provide default no-op stubs that can be overridden only when necessary. Finally, the template-based implementation is even more unfriendly because it doesn't specify required function signatures in the body.

CHAPTER 24

Visitor

Once you've got a hierarchy of types, unless you have access to the source code, it is impossible to add a function to each member of the hierarchy. This is a problem that requires some advance planning and gives birth to the Visitor pattern.

Here's a simple example: suppose you have parsed a mathematical expression (with the use of the Interpreter pattern, of course!) composed of double values and addition operators, for example:

```
(1.0 + (2.0 + 3.0))
```

This expression can be presented as a hierarchy similar to the following:

```
struct Expression
{
  // nothing here (yet)
};

struct DoubleExpression : Expression
{
  double value;
  explicit DoubleExpression(const double value)
    : value{value} {}
};
```

© Dmitri Nesteruk 2022
D. Nesteruk, *Design Patterns in Modern C++20*,
https://doi.org/10.1007/978-1-4842-7295-4_24

```
struct AdditionExpression : Expression
{
  Expression *left, *right;

  AdditionExpression(Expression* const left, Expression* const
  right)
    : left{left}, right{right} {}

  ~AdditionExpression()
  {
    delete left; delete right;
  }
};
```

Given this hierarchy of objects, suppose you want to add some behavior to the various Expression inheritors (we only have two for now, but this number can grow). How would you do it?

Intrusive Visitor

We'll start with the most direct approach, one that breaks the Open-Closed Principle. Essentially, we are going to jump into our already-written code and modify the Expression interface (and, by association, every derived class):

```
struct Expression
{
  virtual void print(ostringstream& oss) = 0;
};
```

In addition to breaking the OCP, this modification hinges on the assumption that you actually have access to the hierarchy's source code – something that's not always guaranteed. But we've got to start somewhere, right? So with this change, we need to implement print() in DoubleExpression (that's easy, so I'll omit it here) as well as in AdditionExpression:

```
struct AdditionExpression : Expression
{
  Expression *left, *right;
  ...
  void print(ostringstream& oss) override
  {
    oss << "(";
    left->print(oss);
    oss << "+";
    right->print(oss);
    oss << ")";
  }
};
```

Ooh, this is fun! We are polymorphically and recursively calling print() on subexpressions. Wonderful, let's test this out:

```
auto e = new AdditionExpression{
  new DoubleExpression{1},
  new AdditionExpression{
    new DoubleExpression{2},
    new DoubleExpression{3}
  }
};
```

```
ostringstream oss;
e->print(oss);
cout << oss.str() << endl; // prints (1+(2+3))
```

Well, this was easy. But now imagine you've got ten classes in the hierarchy (not uncommon, by the way, in real-world scenarios) and you need to add some new eval() operation. That's ten modifications that need to be done in ten different classes. But OCP isn't the real problem.

The real problem is SRP. You see, a problem such as printing is a separate concern. Rather than stating that every expression should print itself, why not introduce an ExpessionPrinter that knows how to print expressions? And, later on, you can introduce an ExpressionEvaluator that knows how to perform the actual calculations. All without affecting the Expression hierarchy in any way.

Reflective Printer

Now that we've decided to make a *separate* printer component, let's get rid of print() member functions (but keep the base class, of course). There's a caveat here: you cannot leave the Expression class empty. Why? Because you only get polymorphic behavior if you actually have something virtual in it. So, for now, let's stick a virtual destructor in there, that will do!

```
struct Expression
{
  virtual ~Expression() = default;
};
```

Now let's try to implement an ExpressionPrinter. Our first instinct would be to write something like this:

```
struct ExpressionPrinter
{
  void print(DoubleExpression *de, ostringstream& oss) const
  {
    oss << de->value;
  }
  void print(AdditionExpression *ae, ostringstream& oss) const
  {
    oss << "(";
    print(ae->left, oss);
    oss << "+";
    print(ae->right, oss);
    oss << ")";
  }
};
```

This code will not compile. C++ knows that, say, ae->left is an Expression, but since it doesn't check the type at runtime (unlike various dynamically typed languages), it doesn't know which overload of print() to call. Too bad!

What can be done here? Well, only one thing – remove the overloads and check the type at runtime:

```
struct ExpressionPrinter
{
  void print(Expression *e)
  {
    if (auto de = dynamic_cast<DoubleExpression*>(e))
    {
      oss << de->value;
    }
```

```
    else if (auto ae = dynamic_cast<AdditionExpression*>(e))
    {
      oss << "(";
      print(ae->left, oss);
      oss << "+";
      print(ae->right, oss);
      oss << ")";
    }
  }

  string str() const { return oss.str(); }
private:
  ostringstream oss;
};
```

The preceding is actually a usable solution:

```
auto e = new AdditionExpression{
  new DoubleExpression{ 1 },
  new AdditionExpression{
    new DoubleExpression{ 2 },
    new DoubleExpression{ 3 }
  }
};
ExpressionPrinter ep;
ep.print(e);
cout << ep.str() << endl; // prints "(1+(2+3))"
```

This approach has a fairly significant downside: the compiler will not check that you *have*, in fact, implemented printing for every single element in the hierarchy.[1] When a new element gets added, you can keep using ExpressionPrinter without modification, and it will just skip over any element of the new type.

It is also important to realize that the type cast checks are order-sensitive: if you have a hierarchy with Parent and Child, you need to check for Child before you check for Parent, and if you screw up the order, you'll never process Child correctly. Now imagine a complicated inheritance hierarchy – your visit() implementation becomes tightly bound to the inheritance ordering within that hierarchy. If this happened automatically somehow, that would be great, but doing it by hand is error-prone and just tedious.

Nevertheless, this approach gives a viable solution. Seriously, it's quite possible to stop here and never go any further in the Visitor pattern: dynamic_cast isn't *that* expensive, and I think many developers will remember to cover every single type of object in that if statement.

What Is Dispatch?

Whenever people speak of visitors, the word *dispatch* is brought up. What is it? Well, put simply, "dispatch" is a problem of figuring out which function to call – specifically, how many pieces of information are required in order to call the correct function.

---

[1] There are, sometimes, benefits to automatically skipping certain types. One such case is when you need to feed the visitor a Null Visitable – an object which does absolutely nothing and does not require anything from any visitor but needs to be there due to, say, API requirements.

Here's a simple example:

```
struct Stuff {}
struct Foo : Stuff {}
struct Bar : Stuff {}

void func(Foo* foo) {}
void func(Bar* bar) {}
```

Now, if I make an ordinary Foo object, I'll have no problem calling func() with it:

```
Foo *foo = new Foo;
func(foo); // ok
```

But if I decide to cast it to a base class pointer, the compiler will not know which overload to call:

```
Stuff *stuff = new Foo;
func(stuff); // oops!
// do we call foo(Foo*) or foo(Bar*)?
```

Now, let's think about this polymorphically: is there *any* way we can coerce the system to invoke the correct overload without any runtime (dynamic_cast and similar) checks? Turns out there is.

See, when you call something on a Stuff, that call *can* be polymorphic (thanks to a vtable) and it can be dispatched right to the necessary component, which in turn can call the necessary overload. This is called *double dispatch* because

1. First you do a polymorphic call on the actual object.

2. Inside the polymorphic call, you call the overload. Since, inside the object, this has a precise type (e.g., a Foo* or Bar*), the right overload is triggered.

Here's what I mean:

```
struct Stuff {
  virtual void call() = 0;
}
struct Foo : Stuff {
  void call() override { func(this); }
}
struct Bar : Stuff {
  void call() override { func(this); }
}

void func(Foo* foo) {}
void func(Bar* bar) {}
```

Can you see what's happening here? We cannot just stick one generic call() implementation into Stuff: the distinct implementations *must* be in their respective classes so that the this pointer is suitably typed.

This implementation lets you write the following:

```
Stuff *stuff = new Foo;
stuff->call(); // effectively calls func(stuff);
```

Classic Visitor

The "classic" implementation of the Visitor design pattern uses double dispatch. There are conventions as to what the visitor member functions are called:

- Member functions of the visitor are typically called visit().

- Member functions implemented throughout the hierarchy are typically called accept().

We can now throw away that virtual destructor from our `Expression` base class, because we've actually got something else to put in there – the virtual `accept()` function:

```
struct Expression
{
  virtual void accept(ExpressionVisitor *visitor) = 0;
};
```

As you can see, our code refers to an (abstract) class named `ExpressionVisitor` that can serve as a base class for various visitors such as `ExpressionPrinter`, `ExpressionEvaluator`, and similar. I've chosen to take a pointer here, but you can use a reference instead.

Now, every single inheritor of `Expression` is now *required* to implement `accept()` in an identical way, namely:

```
void accept(ExpressionVisitor* visitor) override
{
  visitor->visit(this);
}
```

On the other side, we can define the `ExpressionVisitor` as follows:

```
struct ExpressionVisitor
{
  virtual void visit(DoubleExpression* de) = 0;
  virtual void visit(AdditionExpression* ae) = 0;
};
```

Notice that we *must* define overloads for all objects; otherwise, we would get a compilation error when implementing the corresponding `accept()`. We can now inherit from this class to define our `ExpressionPrinter`:

```
struct ExpressionPrinter : ExpressionVisitor
{
  ostringstream oss;
  string str() const { return oss.str(); }
  void visit(DoubleExpression* de) override;
  void visit(AdditionExpression* ae) override;
};
```

The implementation of the visit() functions should be fairly obvious, since we've seen it more than once already, but I'll show it once again:

```
void ExpressionPrinter::visit(AdditionExpression* ae)
{
  oss << "(";
  ae->left->accept(this);
  oss << "+";
  ae->right->accept(this);
  oss << ")";
}
```

Notice how the calls now happen *on* the subexpressions themselves, leveraging double dispatch once again. As for the usage of the new double dispatch Visitor, here it is:

```
void main()
{
  auto e = new AdditionExpression{
    // as before
  };
  ostringstream oss;
  ExpressionPrinter ep;
  ep.visit(e);
  cout << ep.str(); // (1+(2+3))
}
```

Implementing an Additional Visitor

So, what is the advantage of this approach? The advantage is you have to implement the accept() member through the hierarchy *just once.* You'll never have to touch a member of the hierarchy again. For example, suppose you now want to have a way of evaluating the result of the expression. This is easy

```
struct ExpressionEvaluator : ExpressionVisitor
{
  double result;
  void visit(DoubleExpression* de) override;
  void visit(AdditionExpression* ae) override;
};
```

but one needs to keep in mind that visit() is currently declared as a void method, so the implementation might look a little bit weird:

```
void ExpressionEvaluator::visit(DoubleExpression* de)
{
  result = de->value;
}

void ExpressionEvaluator::visit(AdditionExpression* ae)
{
  ae->left->accept(this);
  auto temp = result;
  ae->right->accept(this);
  result += temp;
}
```

The way we handle `AdditionExpression` is a byproduct of an inability to return values from `accept()` and is a little bit tricky. Essentially, we evaluate the left part and cache the value. Then we evaluate the right part (so `result` is set) and then increase it by the value we cached, thereby producing the sum. Not exactly intuitive code!

Still, it works just fine:

```
auto e = new AdditionExpression{ /* as before */ };
ExpressionPrinter printer;
ExpressionEvaluator evaluator;
printer.visit(e);
evaluator.visit(e);
cout << printer.str() << " = " << evaluator.result << endl;
// prints "(1+(2+3)) = 6"
```

And, in the same vein, you can add lots of other different visitors, honoring OCP and having fun in the process. Figure 24-1 shows a class diagram of the different structures we've built.

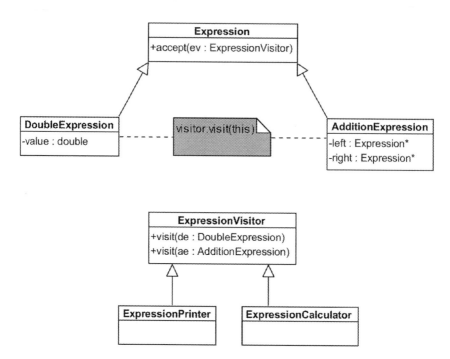

Figure 24-1. *Classic visitor class diagram*

Acyclic Visitor

Now is a good time to mention that there are actually two strains, if you will, of the Visitor design pattern. They are

- **Cyclic Visitor**, which is based on function overloading. Due to the cyclic dependency between the hierarchy (which must be aware of the visitor's type) and the visitor (which must be aware of *every* class in the hierarchy), the use of the approach is limited to stable hierarchies that are infrequently updated.

- **Acyclic Visitor**, which is based on RTTI. The advantage here is the absence of limitations on visited hierarchies, but, as you may have guessed, there are performance implications.

The first step in the implementation of the Acyclic Visitor is the actual visitor interface. Instead of defining a visit() overload for every single type in the hierarchy, we make things as generic as possible:

```
template <typename Visitable>
struct Visitor
{
  virtual void visit(Visitable& obj) = 0;
};
```

We need each element in our domain model to be able to accept such a visitor, but since every specialization is unique, what we do is introduce a *marker interface* – an empty class nothing but a virtual destructor:

```
struct VisitorBase // marker interface
{
  virtual ~VisitorBase() = default;
};
```

This class is empty, but we *will* use it as a parameter in the accept() method in whichever object we want to actually visit. Now, what we can do is redefine our Expression class from before as follows:

```
struct Expression
{
  virtual ~Expression() = default;

  virtual void accept(VisitorBase& obj)
```

```
  {
    using EV = Visitor<Expression>;
    if (auto ev = dynamic_cast<EV*>(&obj))
      ev->visit(*this);
  }
};
```

So here's now the new accept() method works: we take a VisitorBase but then try to cast it to a Visitor<T> where T is the type we're currently in. If the cast succeeds, the visitor in question knows how to visit our type, and so we call its visit() method. If it fails, it's a no-op. It is *critical* to understand why obj itself does not have a visit() that we could call on it. If it did, it would require an overload for every single type that would be interested in calling it, which is precisely what introduces a cyclic dependency.

This implementation of accept() unfortunately needs to be added to every member of the hierarchy, with the dynamic_cast checking for the appropriate type. You can try to simplify this by introducing a macro, but that's really the only thing you can do – it's impossible to introduce some sort of CRTP and still have it all function correctly (try it – make a Visitable<TChild> and see where this gets you).

After implementing accept() in other parts of our model, we can put everything together by once again defining an ExpressionPrinter, but this time around, it would look as follows:

```
struct ExpressionPrinter : VisitorBase,
                           Visitor<DoubleExpression>,
                           Visitor<AdditionExpression>
{
  void visit(DoubleExpression &obj) override;
  void visit(AdditionExpression &obj) override;
```

```
  string str() const { return oss.str(); }
private:
  ostringstream oss;
};
```

Here, we implement the `VisitorBase` marker interface as well as a `Visitor<T>` for every `T` that we want to visit. If we omit a particular type `T` (e.g., suppose I comment out `Visitor<DoubleExpression>`), the program will still compile, and the corresponding `accept()` call, if it happens, will simply execute as a no-op.

In the preceding, the implementations of the `visit()` methods are virtually identical to what we had in the classic visitor implementation, and so are the results. Figure 24-2 shows the structures we've built.

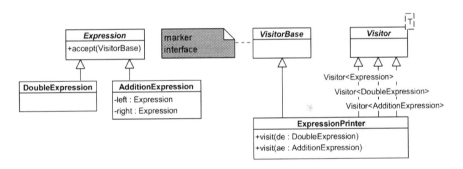

Figure 24-2. *Acyclic Visitor class diagram*

One downside to the Acyclic Visitor is the performance cost associated with `dynamic_cast` being everywhere. Empirical evidence suggests it's about 10× slower than a classic visitor. To lower the performance cost, there are alternatives to RTTI such as various CTTI libraries (e.g., Boost. TypeIndex), which try to adorn classes with compile-time tags that can be used for type comparisons. The performance advantage, when compared to RTTI, is often quite dramatic.

Variants and `std::visit`

While not directly related to the classic Visitor pattern, it's worth mentioning `std::visit`, if only because its name suggests something to do with the Visitor pattern. Essentially, `std::visit` is a way of accessing the correct part of a variant type.

Here's an example: suppose you have an address, and part of that address is a field called house. Now, a house can be just a number (as in "123 London Road") or it can have a name such as "Montefiore Castle." So you can define the variant as follows:

```
variant<string, int> house;
// house = "Montefiore Castle";
house = 221;
```

Either of the two assignments is valid. But what if we decide to print the house name or number? To do this, we can first define a type that has function call overloads for the different types of members inside the variant:

```
struct AddressPrinter
{
  void operator()(const string& house_name) const {
    cout << "A house called " << house_name << "\n";
  }

  void operator()(const int house_number) const {
    cout << "House number " << house_number << "\n";
  }
};
```

Now, this type can be used in conjunction with std::visit(), a library function that applies this visitor to the variant type:

```
AddressPrinter ap;
visit(ap, house); // House number 221
```

It's also possible to define the set of visitor functions in place thanks to some Modern C++ magic. What we need to do is construct a lambda with type of auto&, get the underlying type, compare it using if constexpr, and process accordingly:

```
visit([](auto& arg) {
  using T = decay_t<decltype(arg)>;

  if constexpr (is_same_v<T, string>)
  {
    cout << "A house called " << arg.c_str() << "\n";
  }
  else
  {
    cout << "House number " << arg << "\n";
  }
}, house);
```

Naturally, in addition to constructing and using the lambda in place, it is possible to also save it in a variable for later reuse.

Summary

The Visitor design pattern allows us to add some behavior to every type in a hierarchy of types. The approaches we have seen include

- *Intrusive*: Adding a virtual method to every single object in the hierarchy. Possible (assuming you have access to source code) but breaks OCP.

- *Reflective*: Adding a separate visitor that requires no changes to the objects; uses `dynamic_cast` whenever runtime dispatch is needed.

- *Classic* (double dispatch): The entire hierarchy *does* get modified, but just once and in a very generic way. Each element of the hierarchy learns to `accept()` a visitor. We then subclass the visitor to enhance the hierarchy's functionality.

- *Acyclic*: Just like the Reflective variety, it performs casting in order to dispatch correctly. However, it breaks the circular dependency between visitor and visitee and allows for more flexible composition of visitors.

The Visitor appears quite often in tandem with the Interpreter pattern: having interpreted some textual input and transformed it into object-oriented structures, we need to, for example, render the abstract syntax tree in a particular way. Visitor helps propagate an `ostringstream` (or similar accumulator object) throughout the entire hierarchy and collate the data together.

Index

© Dmitri Nesteruk 2022
D. Nesteruk, *Design Patterns in Modern C++20*,
https://doi.org/10.1007/978-1-4842-7295-4

W, X, Y, Z

Printed in the United States
by Baker & Taylor Publisher Services